D1135492

Regional
ingredients,
recipes and
stories from
Spain

The

Spanish Kitchen

Regional
ingredients,
recipes and
stories from
Spain

The
Spanish Kitchen

CLARISSA HYMAN
2002 GLENFIDDICH FOOD WRITER OF THE YEAR

FOOD PHOTOGRAPHY BY **PETER CASSIDY**

Dedication
To D

First published in 2005 by Conran Octopus Limited, a part of Octopus Publishing Group, 2–4 Heron Quays, London E14 4JP
www.conran-octopus.co.uk
Reprinted in 2005, 2006

Text copyright © Clarissa Hyman 2005; Recipes copyright © Clarissa Hyman 2005; Special photography copyright © Conran Octopus 2005; Travel photography copyright © Clarissa Hyman 2005; Design and layout copyright © Conran Octopus 2005.

The right of Clarissa Hyman to be identified as Author of this Work has been asserted by her in accordance with the Copyright, Designs and Patents Act 1998

All rights reserved. No part of this work may be reproduced, stored in a retrieval system or transmitted in any form or by any means, electronic, electrostatic, magnetic tape, mechanical, photocopying, recording or otherwise, without prior permission in writing of the publisher.
British Cataloguing-in-Publication Data.

A catalogue record for this book is available from the British Library

ISBN 1 84091 478 5

Publishing Director Lorraine Dickey
Commissioning Editor Katey Day
Copy Editor Annie Lee
Art Director Jonathan Christie
Art Editor Alison Fenton
Special Photography Peter Cassidy
Travel Photography Clarissa Hyman
Food Stylist Jacque Malouf
Stylist Chloe Brown
Map Illustrator Russell Bell
Production Manager Angela Couchman

Printed and bound in China

Contents

introduction

Many years ago, I stood on a hillside in Spain and picked a fruit, small and hard as a bullet. It was the first time I had seen olives growing on the tree; the silvery leaves shimmered in a headache-hot, southern light. They gave shade and grace to the raw, oxblood hillside, and they opened my eyes to an old world of secrets and a new world of possibilities. Even today, Spain remains an undiscovered treasure house, full of surprises in food and cooking as in so much else in a country that can be infuriating and contradictory, but is always enticingly complicated, always compelling. The Spanish Kitchen, however, is something of a misnomer – or rather, part of an ongoing debate between national and regional identity that reflects many of the defining tensions of Spanish society. There are, arguably, as many Spanish Kitchens as once there were kingdoms of Spain, and as there are now regions, provinces and cities, *pueblos*

and people: the concept of the *patria chica* (little homeland) remains deeply ingrained, as much a state of mind as physical geography. In my own quixotic journey, in which I travelled thousands of miles, visiting each of the seventeen semi-autonomous regions of Spain, I was constantly struck by an unfailing pride in local ingredients, specialties and in the *cocina de las abuelas* (grandmother's cooking) that seemed the very lifeblood of the peninsular.

Such variation should not, however, come as a surprise in this immense country separated by the Pyrenees from the rest of Europe in a way Italy never was by the Alps; almost, but not quite, part of Africa; tugged towards the Atlantic, pulled back by the Mediterranean. Geogrphical and climatic extremes have shaped regional culture, character and language, as well as ingredients and culinary traditions. The barrier of the high plateaux and mountain *sierras* made internal travel and communication difficult for centuries; even today, there are those who know more about the cooking of Thailand than their regional neighbours. A common classification holds the north is for stews, the south for frying and the centre for roasts, but that too-easy generalisation usually breaks down at the first stop for lunch.

Nonetheless, there are some common culinary threads, such as shared ways of cooking that have helped define a sense of national cooking: grilling over wood and charcoal on the *parrilla* (grid) and *plancha* (griddle), earthenware pots of simmering stews, frying in olive oil, preserving in vinegar and the use of the pestle and mortar. Some dishes have indeed achieved national status, such as tortilla, *flan* and fried potatoes, although others, such as paella and gazpacho, are more questionable holders of the title. More pertinently, individual variations are passionately defended, even when the nuances are as subtle as the difference in theological terms between an angel and an archangel.

As the complicated plot of Spanish history has unfolded, centuries of war, invasion, political turbulence and poverty have been the spur for robust, honest dishes dependent on fresh or expertly preserved ingredients. Each episode in the narrative has left its mark in the Spanish kitchen: saffron and vines from the Phoenicians; olive oil, garlic and vinegar that came with the Romans; pork with the Celts; citrus, rice, sugar, spices and more from the Moorish occupation by Berbers, Arabs and Syrians; revolutionary chillies, chocolate, maize and tomatoes brought back from the New World by the *conquistadores*; even the Church has played its part, and the religious orders have long been the repositories

ABOVE: *LA LONJA*, VALENCIA

of many culinary secrets, including the most exquisite pastries. National pride in cooking has swung from extremes, much as Spain's role in the world has waxed and waned, and it was only in the early part of the twentieth century that the first real attempts were made to record the country's authentic dishes.

Although the pattern is changing, especially in the big cities, there is still a communal timetable in the way meals are structured throughout the day – lunch in the afternoon, as this book was nearly called. Spanish meals are also highly sociable, a convivial but dignified progression through a set sequence of separate dishes. At times, the lack of superfluous frills can seem daunting, but food must always look and taste of what it is. Even the severity of a pile of tiny lamb chops on a plate has a spare elegance; at other times, simple ingredients can be combined in subtle, sophisticated ways or with flashes of colourful brilliance that reflect the pepper-red and saffron-gold of the Spanish flag. The quality of seasonal ingredients that need no tricks in the kitchen is appreciated: the vivid eighteenth century still life paintings of Luis Meléndez are on daily show in the markets of Spain.

At the same time, Spain, like every modern country, has to wrestle with major issues that affect the way it eats: from fishing policies to the difficulties of global trade, pollution, the industrialisation of food, the land and water impact of the vast, plastic tunnel market gardens of south-east Spain, and the increasing dependence on immigrant labour. On a more domestic scale, today paella comes in a packet, cookery magazines are full of Chinese and Italian recipes, and sophisticated kitchen cupboards include Maldon salt, soy sauce and Balsamic vinegar. The concern, of course (and not just in Spain), is that such

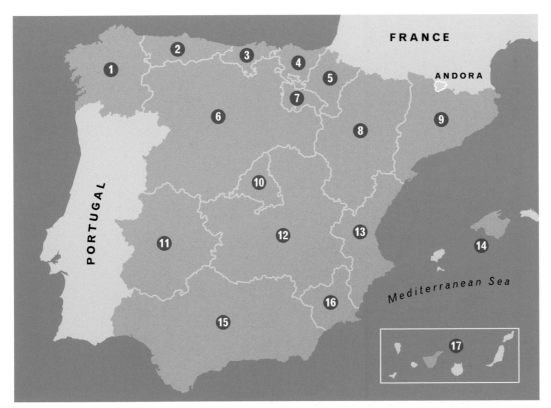

REGIONS OF SPAIN

1. Galicia
2. Asturias
3. Cantabria
4. Basque Country
5. Navarre
6. Castile-León
7. La Rioja
8. Aragón
9. Catalonia
10. Castile-Madrid
11. Extremedura
12. Castile-La Mancha
13. Valencia
14. Mallorca
15. Andalusia
16. Murcia
17. Tenerife

universal lifestyle changes can lead to irretrievable loss, but, as one Spanish food writer told me, sometimes there has to be a necessary exploration of other culinary cultures and fashions before you can fully appreciate your own traditions once again.

Yet there is an excitement in the Spanish kitchen today that is almost unprecedented, fuelled by a gastronomic explosion of global proportions initiated by a group of innovative chefs from the Basque Country and Catalonia. It is the polar opposite of the experience of the nineteenth-century traveller Richard Ford, who wrote 'whenever their cookery attempts to be foreign it.......ends in being a flavourless copy.' The Arzac and Adrìa phenomenon is outside the remit of this book, but these chefs and many others have, more pertinently, over the last few decades drawn attention to a huge array of fine Spanish produce that was unsung, unknown or known for the wrong reasons: inferior, low grade versions. More recently, the fashion for tapas outside of Spain has also helped bring Spanish cooking and ingredients centre-stage.

This book, however, was my own *camino gastronómico*, a way of exploring the deep bond that still exists between produce, people and land. In choosing one classic ingredient from each of the regions, I have tried to present a series of portraits of food and cooking in Spain today that may help towards an understanding of the contemporary Spanish kitchen. My aim has not been to provide an inventory, but a small mosaic of products in the context of their cultivation and history, along with stories and, often, recipes from the people who have been using the ingredient they have grown, reared or fished for generations. The limited cross-section has been difficult to select, but I have tried to include old and (relatively) new; familiar and unexpected; artisan and major industries; small producers who have found a niche for themselves, as well as those struggling to survive in a modern marketplace.

Food, like history, never stands still, but there remain constants. Bread, for instance, still bought fresh, often twice daily. Even though the traditional wood-fired bakeries are declining in number, bread remains one of the most basic, almost mystical, aspects of a Spanish meal. What Dalí called 'the enigma of bread'. Even before the knives and forks, the bread must go on the table; a meal is not a meal without bread, broken with the hands like a sacrament.

Eating in Spain may be a ritual, but it is also a time of enjoyment and sharing. Like the country itself, it has a way of getting under your skin and into your heart.

¡Que aproveche!

Clarissa Hyman
Manchester, 2004

ABOVE: GARLIC SELLER, CHINCHÓN. RIGHT: (TOP LEFT TO RIGHT) DRYING PEPPERS, NAVARRE; PICKLED AUBERGINE SELLER, VALDEPEÑAS; FIESTA MADRID

ANDALUCIA: Málaga raisins

the raisin road

El Corte Inglés, the leading department store, had run out of umbrellas. I had arrived in Málaga on a day of torrential spring rain: collapsed roads, flooded streets, and cascades of water from overloaded awnings. There was only one other thing to do in the capital city of the Costa del Sol – *Costa del Agua*, more like, someone joked – and that was to take refuge in one of the city's venerable *bodegas*, and wait out the storm.

Outside, dripping *malagueños* hurried past, hunched and battered by the gale, like flocks of ugly ducklings. In the packed bar, thick with noise, smoke and the scent of sawdust, arguments broke out as to when the city had last seen such rain – twenty years! No, thirty years at least! You're all wrong, it hasn't rained like this for fifty years, came the assured final bid.

And then, as if in a fairy-tale, the sun broke through, and Málaga became once more a city of beautiful swans. A newly restored city of fine boulevards and gardens, historic buildings and graceful fountains, with the rough and tumble edge of all great Mediterranean ports. Appropriate for a city about which Hans Christian Andersen wrote in the autumn of 1862, 'In no other part of Spain did I feel so happy and so at home as in Málaga.'

After the thunderous clouds, the sudden ferocity of the sunlight hurt the eyes. A patch of sky was as blue as a bullfighter's suit of lights. The air smelt of jasmine and roses, of the salty, tarry sea, of music, adventure and romance. And of wine and grapes and raisins. Which is where our story begins.

OPPOSITE: (LEFT TO RIGHT) MÁLAGA RAISINS; ARTWORK ON A BOX OF RAISINS; THE COURTYARD OF THE MUSEO DE ARTES Y TRADICIONES POPULARES, MÁLAGA ABOVE: BENAMARGOSA, NEAR VÉLEZ-MÁLAGA

'One grape, three products! Raisins, table grapes and wine. That's the first thing you have to learn,' said Javier Aranda Bautista, my guide to *La Ruta de Pasas*, the Raisin Road, that winds through the mountains east of Málaga. We were headed for Axarquía, a wine-making zone also renowned for large, aromatic, sun-dried raisins, once as much a herald of Christmas as Tiny Tim and holly wreaths to homes on both sides of the Atlantic.

The production of sun-dried raisins from *Moscatel* grapes is thought to date back to the Phoenicians; much used in the Moorish cooking of al-Andalus. Under the Muslim Kings of Granada, trade expanded, helped by the opening of the Straits of Gibraltar to Italian ships taking dried fruit and nuts to England and Flanders. By the eighteenth century, Málaga raisins were traded throughout Europe, sought after for their exquisite taste. In 1845, Richard Ford in his *Handbook for Travellers in Spain* commented how superior they were to raisins from Valencia. Even Hans Christian Andersen described how the grapes were laid out to dry on hillsides exposed to sun, but protected from night dew.

The artisan method of production he described has changed very little, with the raisins produced by around 2,000 smallholders, each as individual and obstinate as, well, an Andalucian mule. Javier sees the downside: 'The fragmented structure does not fit into the modern industrial pattern of supermarkets and mass distribution. Most of our raisins go to customers in Madrid and Catalonia; ironically, even in Málaga many people are unaware of the special quality of their own raisins. It's unbelievable!'

Despite the overcast day, the scenery was breathtaking: high ranges, weird rock formations and plunging ravines, where gleaming white Andalucian *pueblos* dripped down distant slopes like melting snow. Although the microclimate is perfect for the vines, protected by the high peaks to the north yet close to the seashore, it was easy to see why grape growing is so difficult; narrow terraces are hacked out of the vertical, black-run slopes, the vines cut low against the stony ground to protect the fruit from the intense summer sun and conserve moisture in the soil. Mules are still used to transport the cut grapes up and down the slopes. One four-legged hero, Romero, has even attained the status of celebrity donkey.

Most families from the nearby towns own a few small plots of land in the mountains planted with vines, where they come each summer for the harvest, but many of the vines are as elderly as the workforce. Still, 'the older the vines, the better the raisins', Javier stoutly explained, although this can mean a lower yield. The grapes ripen early and are hand-cut, although they are now packed in plastic Euroboxes instead of wooden ones, to the chagrin of the growers, who believe the latter are better for flavour.

The grapes are never bleached, dried in artificial ovens nor colour-enhanced, but simply laid out to dry under the burning southern sun. Every house on the steep mountainside has its own parade of distinctive *paseros*, rectangular, slate-covered drying areas, topped by a low triangular wall, that look disturbingly like tilted rows of matrimonial beds.

All the grapes must be hand-turned regularly to ensure even drying, and covered in a sudden downpour by tarpaulin. Within weeks, the magic of sun and air reduces them to wrinkled raisins, each one fleshy, mahogany-dark and luscious, with a long-lasting flavour that captures the very essence of the Muscat grape. But growers such as Juan Jesús Portillo are also bitterly critical of other Euro rulings: 'We cover them in summer so they won't get wet, so why should we wash them when they will lose all flavour and taste like vinegar? Also they say we have to dry the raisins on covered ground, not on slate – but again that way you lose even more flavour. We've been doing it this way for generations, and everyone is quite healthy! No one wants these ridiculous rules.'

Most raisins are now sold as bunches on the vine and are at their best to eat in December and January. Cutting each raisin from the stalk is a delicate, time-consuming business 'best left to the grandmothers!' Hand-packed, the boxes are still a pretty souvenir, though a far cry from the time when nineteenth-century lithographers let their imagination roam free with illustrations of buxom, dark-eyed señoritas, manly *caballeros* and courageous toreadors framed in gold filigree paper.

While it is true that for many Spanish families no Christmas is complete without a box of mellow Málaga raisins, inferior competition has undercut trade, the harvest is laborious and returns uncertain. Modern consumers balk at a few seeds, even though they add a nice little, healthy crunch. Changing patterns of wine consumption have further eroded the vineyards, as has the loss of land to golf courses and holiday villages, plus the increasingly profitable planting of avocados and mangoes on the lower slopes.

'Of course, we don't like to think the future of the Málaga raisin is in doubt,' said Javier, somewhat glumly, 'but it's a difficult, expensive job, and these days people prefer to get their money from building sites rather than agricultural fields.' A pause, then a brave rally: 'But the Regulatory Council is not going to let the Málaga raisin disappear! We now have commercial protection for the name, and are experimenting with growing techniques and varieties that will give a greater yield, as well as extend the season without losing quality, though the drying process must, of course, always remain the same. We are working to develop new markets so the raisins become a gourmet niche product once more. We get very little EU help, we should get more for such an artisan product: the Greeks are much bigger producers and they get much more help!'

Juan Jesús Portillo agreed, 'My sons aren't interested, and with only three hectares you can't get a good living from the prices the raisins fetch. Unless we get more support, the raisins will disappear. These days all the red tape, stupid rules and taxes make it much more complicated. Years ago, you just went to the village with your boxes of raisins and that was that.' Oh dear. We drank a glass of his golden, homemade wine, heady, sweet and raw, instead.

Spanish *alegría* always seems tinged with sadness, part of the struggle for life, but the story is not yet over in the mountains of Málaga. Every fairy-tale needs a happy ending: perhaps Hans Christian Andersen can help. At least, I'd like to think so.

NOTE:Dusky Málaga raisins are remarkable both for their exquisite taste and the fact that they plump up enormously in liquid. However, as they are only available on a seasonal basis, you may have to substitute the best Muscat raisins you can find.

OPPOSITE: 1940's FIESTA POSTER RIGHT: PILAR CISNEROS, LA LOMA RESTAURANT, IZNATE

Veal with Málaga Raisins

Antonio Tovar and Pilar Cisneros (he talks, she cooks) aim to revive traditional Arabic, Jewish and Andalucian dishes at La Loma restaurant in Iznate, high in the mountains near Málaga. They served this dish after first courses of *jamón de Trevélez*, soup with chickpeas and chard, and fried salt cod with garlic. This casserole, they explained, was originally made with lamb, but they believe veal gives better texture and flavour.

SERVES 8

Olive oil (about 100 ml/3½ fl oz)
2 kg/4 lb 8 oz stewing veal (or lamb), cubed
2 large onions, chopped
200 ml/7 fl oz dry white wine
200 ml/7 fl oz Málaga *moscatel* wine (or sherry)
200 g/7 oz Málaga raisins

100 g/ 3½ oz Marcona almonds, pounded in a mortar until very finely chopped (almost but not quite to the point where they would be described as ground)
Salt and white pepper

Pour enough oil into a large deep pan to cover the base, heat and add the veal. Fry until brown, then remove and set aside.

Add the onions and cook over medium-high heat for about 10 minutes until they start to brown, then return the meat to the pan and add enough water to cover, followed by the white wine and half the Málaga wine.

Season, bring up to boiling point, cover and simmer for about 2 hours (you can also use a pressure cooker – a popular pan in the Spanish kitchen).

Add the remaining wine, the raisins and the almonds. Simmer for a few minutes until the raisins swell in size. *¡Perfecto!*

Fish with Spinach, Pinenuts and Raisins

'De la mar el mero, de la tierra el carnero': grouper from the sea, mutton from the land. In other words, an indication of the esteem in which this fine-flavoured Mediterranean fish is held.

This Catalan recipe is usually made with mero or grouper but it can also be made with sea bass, hake or halibut.

SERVES 4

4 thick white fish fillets
Flour, for coating
Olive oil (about 100 ml/3½ fl oz)
1 kg/2 lb 4oz potatoes, peeled and sliced (no more than 1 cm/½ inch thick)
2 large onions, sliced
50 g/1¾ oz pinenuts

2 large garlic cloves, finely chopped
4 large tomatoes, peeled, seeded and chopped
6 spring onions, chopped
50 g/1¾ oz Málaga raisins
25 g/1 oz parsley, chopped
400 g/14 oz spinach, roughly torn
Salt and black pepper

Preheat the oven to 180°C/350°F/Gas Mark 4.

Season the fish and coat in flour, shaking off any excess. Heat plenty of oil in a frying pan over a high heat and briefly seal the fish on both sides. Remove from the pan with a slotted spoon and set aside.

In the same oil, fry the potato slices (in two batches, if necessary) over medium-high heat until just cooked, drain on kitchen paper and place in a large ovenproof dish. Add the onions to the pan and fry for about 10 minutes, until brown at the edges. Add to the potatoes, and place the fish on top.

Lightly fry the pinenuts and garlic in the remaining oil, taking care they do not burn, then stir in the tomatoes, spring onions, raisins and parsley and season well. Cook for a few seconds, then add the spinach. Toss briefly, and as soon as it wilts, remove the pan from the heat. Arrange the spinach mixture over the fish, cover with foil, and bake in the preheated oven for 15 minutes until the fish is cooked through.

ABOVE LEFT: MOUNTAINS NEAR AXARQUÍA

Pork with Málaga Wine, Almonds and Raisins

Almonds and raisins are a naturally harmonious combination, an echo of Moorish times. Spain is the world's second largest almond producer, but of all the varieties grown, Marcona is amongst the finest. The best pork in Spain comes from pigs raised on acorns; in its place substitute rare-breed organic pork (contemporary Moors and Jews can substitute chicken or veal fillets).

Brandy de Jerez is matured in used sherry barrels to give a fine colour and rich, aromatic character. The advertising silhouette of the Osborne Bull, one of the most famous brands, has become a familiar part of the Spanish landscape, perched theatrically on hilltops along every *autopista*.

SERVES 4

2 tenderloins of pork (about 800 g/
   2 lb), cut into medallions
1–2 tablespoons olive oil
1 medium onion, finely chopped
2 garlic cloves, finely chopped
75 g/2¾ oz Málaga raisins

75 g/2¾ oz Marcona almonds,
   flaked and lightly toasted
250 ml/9 fl oz Málaga *moscatel*
   wine (or sherry)
100 ml/3½ fl oz *Brandy de Jerez*
Salt and black pepper

Season the pork with salt and pepper. Heat the oil in a pan and fry the medallions over a medium-high heat for 2–3 minutes on each side until brown. Remove from the pan and set aside.

In the same oil, gently fry the onion for at least 10 minutes. When soft and golden, add the garlic. As soon as the aroma rises, stir in the raisins, almonds, wine, brandy, salt and pepper. Bring to the boil, and simmer for 15 minutes.

Return the pork medallions to the pan and simmer for a further 5 minutes, or until cooked through.

Rum and Raisin *Flan*

The Spanish have a passion for custard-based desserts, but the ubiquitous *flan* can be rubbery hell or velvet bliss. This version is rich and creamy, with the raisins giving an extra dimension of colour, texture and boozy kick. Even if one diner in *casa Clarissa* thought they looked like a layer of dead flies. *¡Por favor!*

SERVES 4

100 g/3½ oz Málaga raisins	200 g/7 oz sugar
30 ml/1 fl oz rum (or Málaga *moscatel* wine or sherry)	1 vanilla pod
	3 large eggs and 2 extra yolks
500 ml/18 fl oz full cream milk	2 tablespoons water

Soak the raisins in the rum for half an hour. Preheat the oven to 180°C/350°F/Gas Mark 4.

Mix the milk and half the sugar in a saucepan. Cut the vanilla pod in half and scrape out the seeds. Add the pods and seeds to the milk, and heat until the sugar dissolves. Take off the heat and remove the pods. Whisk together the eggs and yolks, then blend in the slightly cooled milk.

Prepare the caramel by heating the remaining sugar in a pan over moderate heat, stirring constantly with a wooden spoon. Once it melts it turns quickly from honey to amber, at which point it should immediately be taken off the heat. Add the water – but take care, as the mixture will bubble up. Put back on a low heat, and stir until brown and syrupy.

Pour the caramel into a wetted, metal 1 litre/1¾ pint mould, or four smaller ones, tilting so the syrup covers part of the sides. You need to work fairly quickly before the syrup hardens.

Stir the drained raisins into the custard and pour into the mould. Place in a baking dish large enough to contain the mould, with enough boiling water to come halfway up the sides. Bake for about 40 minutes, until the custard is fairly firm and an inserted knife comes out clean.

Set aside to cool, then chill in the fridge. To serve, cover the mould with a serving plate and carefully invert (it may help to run a palette knife around the edge first).

LEFT: RUM AND RAISIN *FLAN*

ABOVE RIGHT: MÁLAGA RAISINS

Málaga Ice Cream Sundae

From the time of the Moors onwards, snow was taken from the Sierra Nevada, white-capped even in summer, to sweeten with syrup and fruit. This recipe makes a rich and sophisticated dessert, although many Spanish prefer to enjoy their ices during the evening *paseo*, in the fading heat of a long, hot day.

50 g/1¾ oz Málaga raisins	4 large egg yolks
500 ml/18 fl oz Málaga *moscatel* wine or PX sherry	100 g/3½ oz sugar
	Salt
500 ml/18 fl oz full-cream milk	1 teaspoon arrowroot
1 vanilla pod, halved lengthways	

Soak the raisins in 75 ml/2½ fl oz of the wine while you prepare the ice cream.

Put the milk in a heavy saucepan with the vanilla pod and heat until almost boiling. Remove from the heat and leave for 30 minutes to infuse.

Whisk the yolks in a bowl with the sugar and a pinch of salt until the mixture is pale and forms 'ribbons'. Remove the vanilla pod from the milk and gradually whisk the milk into the egg mixture.

Cook the custard in a heavy-based saucepan over very low heat, in the top of a double boiler or in an improvised bain-marie (a saucepan placed over the top of a pan of boiling water), stirring steadily until it has thickened enough to coat the back of a wooden spoon. Remove from the heat, cover and set aside to cool.

Freeze in an ice cream maker, following the instructions, stirring in the raisins when the ice cream is almost firm.

Serve with a wine sauce, made by diluting the arrowroot with a tablespoon of water and heating gently with the remaining wine, stirring until the sauce has thickened. Divide the ice cream between individual serving dishes and drizzle with the wine sauce.

ARAGON: olives and olive oil

'Palomita, palomita,
No levantes tanto el vuelo
Porque te saldrás de España
Y no sabrás volver luego'

'Little dove, little dove,
Don't fly so high,
Because you will fly from Spain
And not find your way home.'

(Traditional *jota* sung during the olive harvest)

river of oil

'Oil, vinegar and salt. In that order,' insisted Carlos. 'The oil has to coat the salad leaves, or the salt falls to the bottom of the bowl.' 'No, that's wrong,' replied Juan. 'Salt first, then the oil and vinegar.' Someone else argued it was salt first, then vinegar and oil. Agustín, chef-patron of the Molí de l'hereu hotel-cum-olive-oil museum in Ráfales, was summoned. 'I only use salt and oil, but you have to drizzle in the oil anti-clockwise.' I was almost sorry I had asked. A simple how-to-dress-the-salad question had turned into a lengthy debate. Still, there was one thing everyone agreed on: it had to be exquisite extra virgin, D.O. olive oil from Bajo Aragón, lightly sweet and gently fruity, with an almond finish and a lack of bitterness or pungency that makes it ideal for use in the kitchen for anything from mayonnaise to frying.

The smooth, subtle oil reflects the golden light that drenches this beautiful, unspoilt region of medieval hilltop villages, craggy sierras, hidden valleys and magical forests full of wild game. The rivers flow into the Ebro, also known as the *oleum flumen* or river of oil. The Romans shipped huge quantities of the precious liquid back home across the Mediterranean. Later, the Arabs improved extraction techniques and, in turn, the industry flourished under the Kings of Aragón, who set a premium on the high quality olive oil. In the early twentieth century, merchants from Marseilles, Nice and Genoa had warehouses in the city of Alcañiz, dominated by the towering mass of the former castle of the Knights of Calatrava, now a luxurious parador. Ironically, most of the region's oil is still exported in bulk to Italy. 'The Italians know it's good, that's why they want it!' was the general consensus. The *aragoneses*, however, always kept back the finest extra virgin olive oil, the DOP oil they are now keen to share with the rest of the world.

OPPOSITE: OLIVES AND OLIVE TREES IN BAJO ARAGÓN. ABOVE: RESERVOIR, BAJO ARAGÓN

The majority of farms are small and family-owned: the olive groves are interspersed with cereals, sweetcorn, and almond and fruit orchards. The gorgeous, late-ripeing yellow peaches of Calanda, in particular, are famous both for their quality and the labour-intensive method of covering each individual fruit with a bag as it grows and ripens. Nonetheless, the names of many villages, such as Calaceite and Beceite, bear witness to their dependence on *aceite*, oil, and in Estercuel, the olive tree is celebrated both in the town's coat of arms and in the monastery of Our Lady of the Olive Grove, named for the medieval vision in which she appeared to a local shepherd from a burning olive tree holding the infant Jesus in her arms. An ancient wooden statue was subsequently found buried in the olive grove, one of Spain's many 'Black Virgins', statues buried centuries before to protect them from the advancing Moorish invasion.

The landscape of Bajo Aragón is still graced by ancient trees – at least, those that escaped the devastations of war, the appalling winter of 1957, and the crazy political machinations of the 1960s when trees were cut down to make way for new industries that never arrived. Happily, the venerable 300-year-old Olivera del Pitongo, near the birthplace of Luis Buñuel, still bears up to 300 kilos of olives each year, harvested in a fiesta attended by dignitaries galore. Lunch consists of a mighty feast of fried eggs, *chorizo*, sausages and spare ribs, and though it may no longer be a time for traditional courting rituals, they still sing the *jotas*, old songs of Aragón. The real harvest is less romantic; a hard, backbreaking job in winter, when there is little daylight and the weather can be bitter, wet and windy.

The oil of Bajo Aragón is produced, mostly, from the native Empeltre olive, a vigorous, upright tree with graceful green and silver leaves perfectly adapted to the limestone soil, low rainfall and climatic challenge of a land where late frosts and fog can descend on the olive groves even in the middle of spring. Suitable land and, hence, total production is small compared to some of the enormous groves of other Spanish regions; but as it gets harder for small farmers to make a living everywhere, growers here know they have to compete in quality, not quantity.

Carlos Estevan Martínez, Secretary of the Regulatory Council for the olive oil of Bajo Aragón, offers the following advice:

1. Keep your olive oil and vinegar in separate cupboards, or the oil will smell of vinegar.

2. Store olive oil in a cool, dark place away from light and heat.

3. Throw away your olive oil can. It is an *"¡instrumento infernal!"* It is never cleaned, just topped up, and the old oil always goes rancid.

4. Never keep your oil for too long. Unlike wine, it does not improve with age.

The elongated fruit, flat on one side and slightly bulging on the other, ripens from early November; curiously all the fruits on a single tree ripen at the same time, and are picked after the olive turns black, which produces the straw-to-old-gold colour and mild, delicate flavour preferred by the *aragoneses*. Many locals leave the picking until even later, with 'battle' traditionally commencing on 8 December, the feast day of *La Inmaculada*, the Immaculate Conception. Recently growers have been encouraged to pick a little earlier, or blend in some Arbequina oil to add a touch more commercial fruitiness and balance.

The olives are hand-picked, using ladders and small sticks to carefully knock the fruit from the branches into nets, thus avoiding undue damage to the tree; increasingly the faster 'umbrella' system is used whereby the olives are mechanically shaken into upturned canvas receptacles. Olives that have fallen to the ground are kept separate, as only those collected from the tree can be used for the extra virgin oil.

The olives are pressed in small mills ranging from those that still use stone wheels and mats to the modern machinery of the award-winning Cooperativa de Valdealgorfa. The basic process, however, remains largely the same, and the most important thing, according to the latter's manager, is speed: 'Farmers bring in their olives each day from the surrounding fields, so they don't travel far. They have to be processed quickly or they'll deteriorate.'

A certain proportion of the olives, selected by size, are destined for table use: small, sweet and dark, they are simply but elegantly brined with salt and wild thyme. Even more remarkable are the 'dead olives', made from fruit frozen on the tree, lightly salted and dressed with oil.

Everywhere else in Spain, olives are called *aceitunas*; here, they are called *olivas*. Because the tree is called an *olivera*, they explained. Contrary, perhaps, but like the *bajoaragoneses*, engaging and singular. Even if they can't agree on the right way to dress a salad.

OPPOSITE (LEFT TO RIGHT) TOWN CENTRE, ALCAÑIZ; JAGANTA ABOVE: BALCONY, ALCAÑIZ

Baked Fish with Olive Oil and Lemon Dressing

In 1745, Juan de Altamiras in *Nuevo Arte de Cocina* gave a recipe for baked bream with bay leaves, garlic and lemon, which he described as 'the best fish in the countries of Aragón'. Despite the sky-high prices, baked fish, especially red sea bream, is a popular dish on Christmas Eve in Madrid, a practice that dates back to the time when it was obligatory to abstain from meat. Traditionally, after the fish, there will be stuffed turkey or capon, red cabbage and sweet almond soup, and *turrón*, almond nougat. Today, more fashionable choices include smoked salmon, shellfish and expensive foreign cheese, all washed down with sparkling *cava*. *¡Felices Fiestas!*

SERVES 4

2 sea bass or red bream, each weighing about 750 g/1 lb 10 oz (or 1 large one), prepared for cooking

Extra virgin olive oil from Bajo Aragón

A handful of fresh bay leaves

1 lemon, sliced, plus 4 tablespoons lemon juice

4 whole garlic cloves, peeled

Sea salt

Black olives from Bajo Aragón

Preheat the oven to 200°F/400°C/Gas Mark 6.

Generously oil a large ovenproof dish and spread the base with bay leaves topped with the sliced lemon. Brush the fish with oil and sprinkle with salt. Place in the dish on top of the bay leaves and lemon and bake for 15–20 minutes, until the skin looks toasted and the fish is cooked through.

Meanwhile heat 6 tablespoons of oil in small pan and gently fry the garlic cloves. When they start to brown, take the pan off the heat, remove the garlic and whisk in the lemon juice.

Fillet the fish and place portions on serving dishes. Pour over the hot oil and lemon mixture, and scatter with a fistful of olives, whole or chopped as you wish.

Lentils with Mushrooms and *Morcilla*

A recipe from Alto Aragón, a wonderfully dramatic area that stretches up to the highest, wildest peaks of the Pyrenees. The whole region is famous for charcuterie, including *morcilla* made with spices, rice and pinenuts, and ham from Teruel, further south. Artisan *anís* from Colungo is a clear spirit of ancient origin, once used as a form of barter. There is only one commercial producer left but they make pretty powerful stuff, guaranteed to add a little *olé* to any dish of lentils.

SERVES 4

400 g/14 oz lentils, pre-soaked if necessary

1 ham bone (optional, but ideally from a *jamón de Teruel*)

2 leeks, finely sliced

1 large onion, finely chopped

Extra virgin olive oil from Bajo Aragón

4 garlic cloves, finely chopped

200 g/7 oz ripe tomatoes, peeled, seeded and chopped

A few bay leaves

150 g/5½ oz wild mushrooms, sliced

200 g/7 oz *morcilla* (Spanish black pudding), sliced thickly

100 g/3½ oz *jamon de Teruel* (or *jamón serrano*), cut into small pieces

50 ml/2 fl oz *anis de Colungo* (or other *anis*)

Salt and black pepper

Put the lentils and ham bone into a covered pan, cover with water, put a lid on the pan and simmer until the lentils are cooked. Drain, reserving the lentils.

Gently fry the leeks and onion in a few tablespoons of oil for at least 10 minutes until soft and starting to brown. Add the garlic, followed by the tomatoes and bay leaves, and fry for another 10 minutes. Add the mushrooms and *morcilla*, and fry for a further 10 minutes.

Add the lentils, jamón and salt to taste. When everything is heated through, sprinkle with the *anís*. Serve with a further drizzle of olive oil. If you prefer more of a 'soup', dilute with some of the cooking stock from the lentils.

LEFT: BAKED FISH WITH OLIVE OIL AND LEMON DRESSING

Chicken *Chilindrón*

As served at the Parador de Alcañiz, the castle fortress of the warrior Knights of Calatrava.

No one really knows what *chilindrón* means, although one school of thought suggests it refers to a game of cards during which the stew was eaten. What is not in question is that it refers to a sauce of onions, red peppers (and sometimes green peppers), tomatoes and garlic. At least, some people include garlic, others don't. Some add ham: one school of thought says that if included at all, ham should be in strips, as it does not release its flavour so well in cubes. Others say the reverse. I told you the *aragoneses* were an argumentative lot.

This is a popular dish throughout northern Spain, made with either chicken or lamb. For the former, some cooks fry the chicken with the skin on, others without, sometimes in quarters, sometimes in smaller pieces – here we go again. However, Juan Barbacil, a Zaragoza-based food writer, offers this little *truco*: 'If you want to fry the chicken without the skin, then save it, crisp in a hot oven and sprinkle over the *chilindrón*.'

Lamb with Lemon and Black Olives

SERVES 4

1 teaspoon ground cinnamon

2 teaspoons *pimentón de la Vera*

2 teaspoons ground cumin

1 kg/2 lb 4 oz shoulder of lamb, cut into bite-sized pieces

1 tablespoon extra virgin olive oil from Bajo Aragón

2 onions, finely chopped

1 small unwaxed lemon, cut into small chunks

150 g/5½ oz black olives from Bajo Aragón

150 ml/5 fl oz white wine

Salt and black pepper

Rub the spices and seasoning into the meat and set aside for at least an hour.

Heat the oil in a large casserole and fry the onion gently for a good 10 minutes until soft and tinged with gold. Add the lamb, turn the heat up to medium-high, and fry until the meat starts to colour. Add the lemon, olives and white wine, then turn the heat down low and cook, covered, for an hour or until the lamb is tender.

NOTE: The lemon is edible – sharp, but not as bitter as you might think, rather like instant preserved lemons.

SERVES 4–6

1 large organic chicken, cut into portions

4–5 tablespoons extra virgin olive oil from Bajo Aragón

1 large garlic clove, peeled and lightly smashed

1 large onion, finely sliced

2 large red peppers, roasted, peeled and seeded

50 g/1¾ oz *jamón de Teruel*, diced

2 kg/4 lb 8 oz ripe tomatoes, peeled, seeded and chopped

1 glass dry white wine (optional)

Salt

Fry the chicken in the olive oil over a medium heat until just golden. Remove and set aside to drain on kitchen paper.

In the same oil, fry the garlic until golden. Remove with a slotted spoon and discard. Add the onion and fry gently for at least 10 minutes, until it becomes soft and transparent. Cut the red pepper into strips and add to the onion, followed by the ham. Cook for a few minutes over a medium heat, then add the tomatoes.

Turn and mix, turn and mix – *'vuelta, vuelta'* – until well combined, then leave to simmer for 30 minutes. Taste, and add a little salt, if necessary.

Add the chicken, cover the pan, and cook on a low heat for 40–50 minutes, until the chicken is tender and the sauce thick. Five minutes before the end, add the wine, if wished.

Note: If using lamb, use more onions and fewer tomatoes.

ABOVE: OLIVE OIL MUSEUM, JAGANTA

RIGHT: CHICKEN *CHILINDRÓN*

ASTURIAS: beans

magic beans

The film director Luis Buñuel once described *fabada*, the legendary bean and pork stew of Asturias, as a dish discovered by a nation of hungry people. By hungry, he implied the hunger of poverty rather than greed – for centuries the beautiful principality of Asturias was a land of impoverished farmers, miners, fishermen and emigrants. Buñuel was right, up to a point, but as Paco Ignacio Taibo in his witty *Brevario de la Fabada* adds, 'The history of the *fabada* is the history of a country's prosperity…it is the product of a more recent middle class that could enjoy the selfish pleasures of the kitchen and contemplate the world with an easy, unruffled digestion.' Before the nineteenth century, he comments, no Asturian peasant would waste their precious beans, ham, chorizo and black pudding on one lavish, blow-out meal; rather, they would eke them out through the week in old country dishes such as the equally iconic *pote asturiano*.

Few dishes inspire such reverence and passion as the mighty, gut-busting *fabada*, whose flatulent potency is jokingly held responsible for the defeat of the Arab armies at Covadonga in 722 by the fearless Asturian guerrilla fighters. The classic format is strict: as Taibo witheringly insists, *fabada* should contain neither pigs' ears, garlic, onion nor spices, extraneous ingredients that have crept in as a result of incursions from 'the *fabada's* enemies' to compromise its traditional integrity and simplicity.

Fabada, he rightly claims, does not travel (except, perhaps, in tins, but even then…). It can be imitated but never truly reproduced. A true *fabada* must be made with Asturian pork and beans – even the water must be Asturian for the taste to be exactly right. Above all, the beans must be the unique *fabas de la granja*, large, white bullet-shaped beans of the species *Phaseolus vulgaris*.

The beans are a wonder: double their sized once cooked, they remain whole, firm and smooth, with a delicate, buttery taste, velvet texture and a skin that virtually disappears in the mouth. They also possess a magical ability to absorb the taste of the other ingredients. Asturians describe them as *agradecida*, grateful for the flavour.

Traditionally beans were an important source of nourishment, one of the crops grown on the self-sufficient mixed smallholdings or *caserías* characteristic of the region. Cultivation is based around the coastal areas, rolling inland valleys and fertile river banks where the climate is mild, damp and misty; the beans need sun and rain, but not too much of either. The beans, which grow several metres high, are supported either by companion corn plants, iron rods, or strings and nets. Every method has its advantages and disadvantages; it's a regular topic of conversation among local bean farmers.

Yet even in this emerald-green slice of Spain, separated from the Castilian *meseta* by soaring peaks, there are changes under the placid surface of rural life. Asturias has wonderful cheeses and the best milk in Spain, but production has fallen as a result of competition from Eastern Europe. The market has also been hit by the import of cheap beans from Bolivia; no little irony, as the ancestors of the *fabas* were

OPPOSITE: (LEFT TO RIGHT) BEAN PLANT IN FLOWER; ASTURIAN BEAN FIELDS; STREET SCULPTURE IN OVIEDO

ABOVE: *POTE ASTURIANO*, CASA LULA

originally imported from the New World by Asturian sailors and *indianos*, settlers who returned home to build stylish houses and plant palm trees. Some of the beans on sale in Oviedo, as I was sternly informed, have leathery skin, a grainy, floury taste, and fail to swell after soaking. Only the symbol of the Regulatory Council guarantees that each charming fabric bag contains the real thing.

José Manuel García is a cheerful, bearded ex-professional cyclist and free spirit who now farms organic beans, potatoes, tomatoes and apples near Otur. The wind was blowing off the sea with a salty scent when we found him hand-weeding between the young plants, and he stopped to reflect on changing times. 'My parents used to have cows, but had to give up. I've carried on with the crops, but have switched to organic because it is a philosophy I deeply believe in. Yes, farming is hard, and many people don't want it for their children. But life is hard for everyone, so you must believe in what you do and get satisfaction from that.'

The seeds, which are kept from year to year, selected by size and colour, are usually sewn in May in a shallow trench, 'so the beans can see the farmer go home, as we say!' He also ploughs the fields by hand, but María José Valdés, further down the coast, where the land drops abruptly from high cliffs into the sea, uses a horse to work the family plot: historically, bean-growing has always been women's work. In October the beans are picked, either pod by pod if the weather is good, or by cutting the whole plant to be dried in the raised barns or *hórreos*, built of stone and chestnut wood, that dot the Asturian landscape like gnomic garden sheds.

Like almost every Asturian, María José makes *fabada* at least once a week, as well as beans with shellfish. 'Everyone loves beans in my house, even my two young daughters. We never tire of them!'

ABOVE: (LEFT TO RIGHT) ATLANTIC COAST NEAR PUERTO DE VEGA; RESTAURANT SIGN, LOS PISONES
OPPOSITE: CAFÉ-BAR, OVIEDO

La fabada

The main components of the classic *fabada* are almost impossible to find outside Asturias, and although it is possible to make an approximation, you should really visit this beautiful part of Spain instead, enjoy it *in situ*, and reflect on the qualities of dishes that do not, and perhaps should not, 'travel'. Just pack an iron stomach; after a plateful of *fabada*, you won't be travelling anywhere either.

According to Paco Ignacio Taibo, *la fabada* must include only beans (*fabas asturianas*) and their essential 'companions': chorizo, *morcilla* (black pudding), *tocino* (salted belly pork), *lacón* (cured front leg and shoulder of pork), a ham bone, saffron, salt and water, or 'it goes against the simple dignity of the opulent *fabada*'. An explanation, perhaps, why *fabada* has also been described as 'a pig resting on a bed of beans'.

For the record, this is also the way that Mayte Alvarez Arias makes it at Casa Lula in El Crucero near Tineo, a family restaurant that now seats 350 diners and which celebrated its seventy-fifth anniversary in 2000. Mayte, who took over the running of the restaurant from her mother-in-law, is a member of the unique *Club de Guisander as* (literally stew-makers), a sisterhood of cooks renowned for their prowess at the stove who are dedicated to keeping alive the recipes and traditions of the matriarchal Asturian kitchen.

'One kilo of beans serves between 8 and 10 people. Soak them overnight, rinse well and place in a deep, two-handled pan. Cover with fresh water and put over a low heat. Add pricked links of homemade *morcilla* and chorizo. Half cover the pan, and when the liquid just reaches boiling point, add a little bit of cold water to cool it down. This "surprises" the beans, keeps them tender and stops them breaking up.

'Add some large pieces of home-cured *tocino* and *lacón*, and a meaty bone (ideally *hueso de butiecho*, part of the pig's backbone). Make sure the beans are always covered with water, and as they simmer, keep skimming the foam from the surface, adding a little more cold water every time the liquid starts to boil. The *lacón* gives salt, but you can test later to see if it needs more. Give the pan a shake from time to time to stop the beans from sticking, but don't stir (that's why you need a pan with two handles so it doesn't splash). If you really have to stir, then use a wooden spoon. The local Asturian water is crucial – we had to take bottled water when we were invited to cook it in Barcelona!

'Cover and simmer for about an hour. The time depends on the quality of the beans; if they're good, they'll cook faster than poor, thick-skinned ones. Halfway through the cooking, add two packets of saffron. I put them on top of the lid of the *fabada* to warm and release the flavour first, then crush them a little in the packet before adding gently.

'Once it is made it needs to stand for half an hour to "settle" and let the juices thicken. If it is still not thick enough, you can purée some beans and return them to the pot. *Fabada* is best made the day before you need it. Either serve the meat on a side platter or cut up small pieces for each plate. This is *cocina de cariño* – Asturian soul food. No one ever tires of it.'

GENERAL NOTE: *Fabas* are unique, but if necessary you can substitute other white beans. The taste and texture, however, will be quite different.

Asturian Beans with Partridge

And they lived happily ever after... or, in Spanish, *fueron felices y comieron perdices* – they were happy and dined on partridges. In Spain, happiness is partridge-shaped, and it is the country's most popular game bird, whether specially reared or shot in the wild when the season opens in October. Chicken or guinea fowl can be substituted in this filling winter stew.

SERVES 4

400 g/14 oz *fabas asturianas*	2 bay leaves
2 red-legged partridges, cut in half	Freshly grated nutmeg
3 tablespoons olive oil	2 large garlic cloves
1 large onion, finely chopped	25 g/1 oz fresh parsley
1 green pepper, finely chopped	2 tablespoons sherry vinegar
3 large tomatoes, skinned, seeded and roughly chopped	4 tablespoons white wine
	Salt

Soak the beans in water overnight. Drain, cover with fresh water and put over a low heat. As the water starts to come to the boil, add a small glass of cold water. The beans must always be covered with water, so add another glass from time to time as the cooking liquid evaporates. The cold water 'surprises' the beans and keeps them tender. Once the beans are cooked, after about an hour, add salt. Drain and set aside.

Season the partridges with salt and fry in hot oil so they brown on all sides. Place in a deep casserole along with any remaining oil. Add the onion, green pepper and tomatoes to the pot, with the bay leaves and nutmeg.

Put the garlic, parsley and some salt into a mini-processor and blitz until finely chopped. Blend in the vinegar and white wine and add this mixture to the casserole. Cover and simmer for about 20 minutes, until the partridges are cooked (you will have to adjust cooking times if using other birds). Add the beans and cook for another 10 minutes, until they are heated through.

Asturian Bean Salad

A modern recipe that shows the beans at their finest.

SERVES 4–6

400 g/14 oz *fabas asturianas*	2 shallots, finely chopped
250 g/9 oz salad leaves	Olive oil
100 g/3½ oz *panceta*, cubed or cut into slivers	Vinegar
	Salt and black pepper

Soak the beans and boil according to the directions for Asturian Beans with Partridge. Drain and set aside. Arrange the salad leaves in a serving bowl.

Fry the *panceta* in a non-stick pan until crisp. Drain and add to the salad along with black pepper and a little salt. Add the beans and shallots and dress with oil and vinegar to taste. Toss the salad gently, and serve straight away.

LEFT: ASTURIAN BEAN SALAD

ABOVE: ASTURIAN FARMHOUSE NEAR PUERTO DE VEGA

Asturian Beans and Shellfish

This gloriously messy dish comes from another member of the *Club de Guisanderas*, Elena Gutiérrez Díaz, of Los Pisones restaurant, near Gijón. Asturians, like most Spanish, are very knowledgeable about the quality of shellfish, and are willing to pay a high price for the best without a second thought. Any available shellfish can be used in this recipe – and don't be afraid to use your hands to tackle the seafood. It's the only way.

SERVES 4

400 g/14 oz *fabas asturianas*

1 small onion, very finely chopped

100 g/3½ oz courgette or squash, very finely chopped

1 sprig of fresh parsley, very finely chopped

2 small crabs, chopped in half

1 spider crab, quartered

4 large crayfish or king prawns

8 clams

1 garlic clove, chopped

3 tablespoons olive oil

1 tablespoon *pimentón de la Vera*

Salt

Soak and cook the beans according to the instructions for Asturian Beans with Partridge, adding the onion, courgette and parsley to the water. Two thirds of the way through, add the seafood, keeping the pot at a gentle simmer. Stir carefully with a wooden spoon.

Fry the garlic gently in the oil until golden. Add the *pimentón*, stir for a few seconds and pour on to the beans. Stir and, keeping the heat low, cook for a little longer, and add salt to taste. Remove from the heat and leave to stand for 10 minutes before serving.

ABOVE: FISH MARKET, PUERTO DE VEGA

RIGHT: ASTURIAN BEANS AND SHELLFISH

BASQUE COUNTRY:
bonito del norte

the *bonito* coast

Six thirty in the morning. The boats had landed the catch on the dark Bermeo quayside only a few hours earlier, and the buyers were already inspecting the fish. It had been a heavy, sultry August night, and more rain was in the air; underfoot the ground was slippery, streaked with water and blood. There was little conversation. A quick, practised glance at the *bonito del norte*, and a few, muted greetings.

The *bonito* were brilliant in the harsh, artificial light, tight as a drum, small and streamlined as scud missiles. Like a Rothko canvas, a slash of bright blue separated the backs, black as thunder, from the shiny, silver bellies. Their long fins were stiff and sharp, designed to slice the waves like surfboards in the search for food, a temperate climate and spawning grounds.

Half an hour later the auction was under way, as it has been since the 1500s, although today's buyers sit at numbered desks before an electronic screen, designed like a roulette wheel. The auction is conducted in reverse; the price starts high, and drops. The room was hushed, intense. Dealings were still in pesetas – 'easier to calculate small differences of price' – but we were talking serious money. Seasonal *bonito del norte* is highly prized in Spain, valued for its delicate white meat by both the fresh fish market and the canning industry for which Bermeo has long been famous. Compared to the increasingly endangered *atún rojo*, or bluefin tuna, it is as veal to beef.

Outside, the day was colouring in the small, solid town; the paintbox colours of the trawlers stood out against the red rooftops, switchback mountain slopes and granite sea, old as the Basque people, old

OPPOSITE: (LEFT TO RIGHT) FRESHLY CAUGHT *BONITO*; THE OLD PORT, BERMEO
ABOVE: *BONITO* FISHING BOAT, BERMEO

as time. Bermeo was not only a pioneer of the nation's whaling fleet but, in 1351, signed a treaty with England that first established the principle of freedom on the high seas. Later, the ships for Columbus's second voyage were built and largely crewed from here, a story well documented in the Museo del Pescador, housed in a fifteenth-century tower by the Old Port.

Thunnus alalunga, otherwise called *bonito del norte*, the Atlantic white tuna, albacore or, in Basque, *egaluze*, is one of the smallest of the tuna family. From July to October, when they are at their best, the Bermeo fleet sets out to follow the schools through the Cantabrian Sea. *Bonito* has mysterious migratory patterns. The previous year the catch had been poor, and although more fish – and bigger ones, better for canning purposes – had arrived early in the Bay of Biscay from the Azores this year, no one knew whether they would depart earlier too.

The *bonito* are caught in one of two traditional ways: with hooked sticks, live bait and small nets or with long rods and a towed network of lines like a fairground ride, a surface trawling system that dates from the sixteenth century. Other fleets still use controversial mid-water trawl nets, although EU drift net fishing, darkly described locally as 'death nets', is more tighly controlled. Once landed, the fish are killed rapidly with a blow to minimize bloodstains and the release of lactic acid from muscle spasm, both of which can spoil flavour and texture. Juveniles are returned to the sea. Experienced buyers such as José Ramón Ruiz de Azúa, co-owner of the canning firm of Arroyabe, know which boats handle the catch with the greatest care.

Arroyabe is a small family business that dates back over a century; the cannery is modern but still artisan, unlike the large, industrialized plants in other parts of Spain that depend heavily on imported, frozen, raw and pre-cooked skipjack and yellowfin tuna. Canning developed as an adjunct to the salted anchovy preservation industry started along the coast by immigrant Sicilians. *Bonito* appear in the Cantabrian Sea after the anchovy schools leave, and during the summer the small factories would preserve it in vinegar. As technology improved and tastes changed, the vinegar was replaced by oil.

The fish is processed within twenty-four hours, never frozen. The *ventresca*, the creamy, richest and most prized cut, is skilfully extracted from the belly just below the gills, and boiled separately from the larger fillets. According to José's daughter Elena, the cooking time is a matter of judgement: 'How long you cook it depends on many factors such as size. It must be neither undercooked nor overcooked, or it gets too dry to can. You have to cook it *a punto!*' The *bonito* is dexterously filleted, skinned and trimmed on the all-female production line, before it is carefully packed in cans or jars, covered in olive oil and sealed.

In one of the town's lively bars, overlooking the harbour where the day had started many hours earlier, I ate canned *bonito* the local way with chopped onions, green peppers and a splash of vinegar. More small plates of *pintxos* arrived. More beer. More conversation and good-humoured bustle. The older men wear the *chapela*, the black Basque beret. As one of Hemingway's characters in *The Sun Also Rises* remarks, 'These Basques are swell people.' And the *bonito's* pretty darned good as well.

ABOVE: BERMEO RIGHT: (TOP LEFT TO RIGHT) GUERNICA; BERMEO; GUGGENHEIM MUSEUM, BILBAO

Basque *Bonito* Dip

Versatile, hard to categorize but with a distinctive Basque identity, this is somewhere between a snack, starter, dip, spread, stick-your-spoon-in-as-you-pass-the-bowl...and good to eat any time of day.

SERVES 6–8 AS A STARTER

1 large onion, finely chopped

3 green peppers (or a mixture of colours), finely chopped

2 fat garlic cloves, finely chopped

2 tablespoons olive oil

175 g/6 oz mixed green and black olives, pitted and chopped

50 g/1¾ oz capers, drained

400 g/14 oz tinned tomatoes in rich juice

2 tablespoons tomato purée

425 g/15 oz tinned *piquillo* peppers, drained and cut into small pieces

1 tablespoon sherry vinegar

225 g/8 oz tinned *bonito* (or other tuna), drained and flaked

Salt and black pepper

Toasted country bread (to serve)

Gently fry the onion, green peppers and garlic in the oil in a deep saucepan for about 15 minutes, until soft.

Add the olives, capers, tomatoes (plus juice) and tomato purée, and cook gently for 5 minutes. Add the *piquillo* peppers and cook for five more minutes .

Stir in the vinegar, followed by the *bonito*. Check the seasoning, (it will probably need no extra salt but quite a bit of pepper), simmer a little longer and leave to cool. Chill in the fridge, preferably leaving overnight for the flavours to settle, before serving with slices of toasted country bread.

Fried *Bonito* with Prawns

This recipe comes from Galicia, and is also good with a little *pimentón de la Vera* added to the sauce. Many Spanish cooks use *harina para rebozar*, a coarse-milled flour, when coating fish to be fried, but ordinary flour works perfectly well.

SERVES 4

1 kg/2 lb 4 oz ripe tomatoes, peeled and seeded

1 medium onion

1 medium red pepper, seeded

100 g/3½ oz *jamón serrano*

1 large garlic clove

25 g/1 oz fresh parsley

About 8 tablespoons olive oil

4 fresh *bonito* or other tuna steaks, salted

Flour

12 cooked prawns (with or without shell, as preferred)

Preheat the oven to 180°C/350°F/Gas Mark 4.

Finely chop the tomatoes, onion, red pepper, ham, garlic and parsley in a food processor. Heat half the oil in a frying pan, add the tomato mixture, and fry gently for 30 minutes. Transfer to a heatproof dish.

Lightly coat the fish in flour and fry in the remaining oil until gold on both sides. Place in the dish on top of the sauce, drizzling over any oil left in the frying pan.

Bake in the preheated oven for 10 minutes, and decorate with the prawns before serving.

LEFT: BASQUE TUNA DIP

ABOVE RIGHT: *BONITO* FISHING BOAT, BERMEO

To make the stock, put the reserved trimmings into a large pan with 2 litres/3½ pints of water, the sliced onion and the white wine. Bring to the boil and simmer for 30–40 minutes. Strain and reserve.

Simmer the *choricero* peppers in water for about 20 minutes until soft. Drain, reserving a glass of the liquid. Slit the peppers open and remove the seeds, then scrape off the inner flesh and discard the outer skin. Set aside.

Cut the potatoes into small chunks, using the cut and 'break' method (cut at an angle into the potato and tear/gouge out a chunk – this helps the potato release its starch while cooking). Set aside.

Heat the oil in a deep stew pot and add the chopped onions. Cook for 5 minutes, then add the green pepper, remaining garlic and two pinches of salt. Leave to to cook on a medium-low heat for 30 minutes, until the onions are soft and tinged with gold.

Add the potatoes and turn them frequently, but gently, with a wooden spoon for about 10 minutes. Add the *choricero* flesh and the reserved cooking liquid, plus the *pimentón* and stock. Bring to the boil, and simmer for 30 minutes or until the potatoes are soft. Take off the heat and leave to settle for half an hour before serving.

Add the *bonito* and the tomato sauce. Bring to the boil and simmer for a few minutes until the fish is just cooked.

Kiko's *Marmita*

Kiko Martínez Nates of Laredo in Cantabria gave me the recipe for his winning dish in the town's annual *marmita* competion. The same dish, of which there are many versions, goes by the name of *marmitako* in the neighbouring Basque Country, and is said to have been cooked originally by fishermen on board their boats. Although best made with *bonito*, it can also be made with other tuna.

SERVES 8–10

1.5 kg/3 lb 4 oz fresh *bonito*, rinsed well	6 dried *choricero* peppers, rinsed and soaked in hot
1 small bunch of fresh parsley, finely chopped	water for 30 minutes (or other dried sweet chilli pepper)
4 large garlic cloves, chopped	12 medium potatoes, peeled
3 large onions, 1 sliced and 2 finely chopped	6 tablespoons olive oil
4 slugs of white wine	1 large green pepper, chopped
	1 teaspoon *pimentón de la Vera*
	2 tablespoons tomato sauce
	Sea salt

Cut the tuna into large cubes, reserving some of the skin, bone and trimmings. (You only need a few trimmings, otherwise the stock will be too strong.) Put the tuna into a bowl with the parsley, half the garlic and a little salt and set aside.

Marinaded *Bonito Brochetas*

This can be made with both fresh *bonito* and tuna. No olive oil is used in the marinade; only lemon flavours the fish, along with a hint of spices.

SERVES 4

1 kg/2 lb 4 oz fresh *bonito* (or other tuna)	2 red onions, quartered
2 juicy lemons, squeezed	3 peppers, cut into large pieces
4 garlic cloves, finely chopped	100 g/3½ oz cherry tomatoes
1 tablespoon ground cumin	Fresh parsley, chopped
	Salt

Cut the *bonito* into cubes (about 4 cm/1½ inches). Mix together the lemon juice, garlic, cumin and salt to taste, and marinate the *bonito* in the mixture for at least 30 minutes.

Skewer the *bonito* alternately with the onions, peppers and tomatoes and cook under a fierce grill or on a griddle for 2–3 minutes on each side. Sprinkle with parsley before serving.

ABOVE: KIKO, FRIENDS AND *MARMITA*
RIGHT: MARINADED BONITO KEBABS

CANTABRIA: anchovies

'La primavera se ve llegar
Se va el invierno
Frío y cruel
Se va el chicharro
Se va el verdel
Llega el bocarte
Se tira el arte
Duro con el!'
(Traditional Cantabrian fishermen's song)

little rascals

Kiko Martínez Nates, fast-talking, gregarious and permanently plugged into his mobile phone, burst into a traditional song that roughly translates as 'Spring is coming, as the cold, cruel winter departs. The horse and chub mackerel are leaving, but the anchovies are arriving, so let's get out our nets and go catch them!'

We were in the El Marinero restaurant in the middle of Laredo, an attractive small port and popular holiday town on the Cantabrian coast, near the elegant, *fin-de-siècle* resort of Santander. I had come to learn about anchovies, but was also taking a crash course in the art of the apéritif hour. Over sea-salty *percebes* or goose-necked barnacles, my convivial hosts explained, 'This is the most important social ritual of the day, when everyone gets together after work to snack a little, drink a little and talk a lot.' They

were taking my instruction seriously, and as far as I could see, apéritif hour not only arrived twice a day but occupied several hours in between as well. Even if a bit past its heyday, Laredo was certainly living up to its old, party-going reputation as the Spanish answer to St Tropez.

If fish can be described as having a personality, then there is a certain resemblance between Laredo's finest and the shoals of anchovies that arrive off the coast each year. Locally called *bocartes*, a word play on their prominent jawbone or 'big mouth', the little blue-black fish swim in sociable packs and could be said to have a bit of a rowdy spirit, rather like gangs of cheeky urchins, a trifle boastful but wholly engaging. Or maybe that's just the gin and tonic speaking (part of my Cantabrian education also included the amount of lemon peel essential for the perfect sundowner. The Spanish insist they know best.)

OPPOSITE: (LEFT TO RIGHT) BEACH, SANTANDER; FISHING BOAT, LAREDO

ABOVE: FISHING BOAT, LAREDO

What is not in dispute is that richly flavoured, meaty Cantabrian anchovies are rightly renowned, preserved in tins by an industry that was developed in the late nineteenth century by Sicilian immigrants using salting techniques that date back to the Romans. Their descendants still own some of the factories in the towns of Laredo, Santoña and Colindres. No external signs are needed; a characteristic pungent smell acts as an address.

St Joseph's Day, 19 March, is the traditional start of the anchovy fishing season, when the fish arrive in the Bay of Biscay to feed on the plankton-rich waters. Early fishing boats were shaped like long rowboats, and were also used for racing; at night, flaming torches would attract the schools of little fish. Nowadays, the inshore fishing is mostly from small boats using purse seine nets. The fishermen say that anchovies caught with drift nets come to the factory 'tired', due to the battering they receive during capture.

The artisan preserving process also remains little changed. The catch is treated with great care, in order to keep each little fish perfectly intact. Once landed, the anchovies are placed in large buckets of brine to drain the blood. The head and guts are removed, and the largest fish are packed in sea salt to mature as salted anchovies. The remainder will be canned in oil, but are first pressed in star-shaped formation in barrels, layered with salt and covered with heavy weights. The curing, which gives the fish its characteristic red-brown colour, takes 6–8 months and is like ageing wine in barrels: fat, water and salt content, as well as the weather, can all affect the process.

ABOVE: HARBOUR, LAREDO OPPOSITE: (LEFT TO RIGHT) A LAREDO FISHERMAN; SANTANDER PROMENADE

'You want to know the best way to eat anchovies? On their own! A little bread, a little wine – that's all you need.' Diego Velasco, Santander

The next step is to skin the fish, either by hand or by a combination of hand and machine. Women workers deftly cut off the tail and fins, wrap the fish in cloth squares, and either twist the cloths by hand or spin them in a centrifuge to remove excess water. Once the fish are clean and dry, another group of women meticulously remove the dorsal spine and any remaining bones, handling the fish as carefully as brain surgeons. The final step is to separate and trim each firm fillet, before they are hand-packed in symmetrical patterns in containers which are then filled with oil.

The Spanish humorist Enrique Jardiel Poncela once declared that if the Czars had ever tasted an anchovy sandwich they would never have bothered to invent caviar, but the industry nonetheless has had its reverses. In the 1960s, in particular, there was a sharp fall in anchovy numbers, which resulted in factory closures; today the fishing fleet faces pressure from the European Commission to reduce the total allowable catch in order to rebuild stocks. Competitively priced but inferior anchovies from countries such as Chile and Morocco are imported for processing, but only the tins labelled Cantabrian anchovies guarantee locally caught fish. Then you know they've been swimming within sight of the beautiful, welcoming region around Laredo that boasts the best beach in Spain. *¡Vale!* I kept my promise, guys! The next round's on you.

NOTE: At no point are Cantabrian anchovies heat-treated, so in a sense the curing process continues after the fish are canned; therefore they are defined as semi-perishable and tins should be kept in a cool place, regularly turned over.

Anchovy Tapas

A recent survey found that Spain has seven bars for every 1,000 people, twice as many as the European average. The Spanish, however, never drink without a little something to eat, whether it is on a plate, a cocktail stick or a piece of bread or toast. The first *pintxo (tapa)* in north-west Spain is said to have been *la gilda*, an anchovy preserved in oil, a pickled chilli and a green olive skewered on a cocktail stick, created in 1941 at the Bar Martínez in San Sebastián.

ANCHOVIES LAREDO STYLE
Lightly combine 8 chopped, tinned Cantabrian anchovy fillets, 1 roughly chopped hard-boiled egg, a handful of chopped olives and capers and a splash of sherry vinegar.

KIKO'S CANAPES
Slice some bread sticks fairly thinly and spread with a little tomato purée. Add a thin slice of cheese (Manchego is fine), top with a tinned Cantabrian anchovy and bake briefly in a hot oven.

You can also top rectangles of ready-made puff pastry with sautéd spring onions and Cantabrian anchovies.

ANCHOVY, CHEESE AND OLIVES
Impale chunks of Manchego cheese on toothpicks with a few coiled, tinned Cantabrian anchovies and green olives stuffed with pimiento.

FRESH ANCHOVIES FROM EL MARINERO
Sprinkle fresh anchovy fillets with a little salt and fry gently on both sides in olive oil. Remove and layer over thin slices of toasted bread. Add finely chopped garlic and fresh parsley and a little white wine to the pan, fry briefly and pour over the fish. Serve at once.

ANCHOVIES WITH LEMON
Drench fresh anchovy fillets with lemon juice and season with salt and pepper. Chill for at least 2 hours. Drain, drizzle with olive oil, sprinkle with chopped fresh parsley and marinate for another hour before serving.

ABOVE: HARBOUR CAFÉ, LAREDO

LEFT: ANCHOVY TAPAS

Lentil and Anchovy Salad

Spain has a wonderful range of dried legumes, which were for centuries as important to the Spanish diet as bread itself, to the extent that they were sometimes known as 'poor man's meat'. For this recipe, try to find the lovely, light green lentils of La Armuña, from the province of Salamanca.

SERVES 4–6

500 g/1 lb 2 oz lentils	12 tinned Cantabrian anchovy
200 g/7 oz onions, finely	fillets
chopped	
500 g/1 lb 2 oz tomatoes, skinned	FOR THE DRESSING:
and seeded	½ tablespoon mustard
100 g/3½ oz black olives, pitted	Juice of half a lemon
25 g/1 oz fresh parsley, chopped	50 ml/2 fl oz olive oil
	Salt

Rinse the lentils in cold water and place in a saucepan. Cover with twice their volume of salted water, bring to the boil and add the onion. Simmer for 20–30 minutes or until tender.

Turn the lentils and onions into a colander and rinse briefly in cold water. Drain well. Transfer the lentils into a serving dish and stir in the tomatoes, olives, and parsley.

Just before serving, make the dressing: mix the mustard and a little salt with the lemon juice and whisk in the olive oil until the mixture thickens. Gently toss the salad with the dressing and decorate with the anchovies, arranged in a criss-cross pattern on top (silvery side upwards).

Deep-Fried Anchovies with Garlic and Parsley

To deep-fry fish successfully, you need a large pan and plenty of very hot oil – and the patience not to fry too many at a time.

SERVES 4–6

About 20 fresh anchovies	Two eggs, beaten
4 large cloves garlic	Breadcrumbs (about 150g/5½ oz)
25g/1oz fresh parsley	Oil, for deep-frying
Olive oil	Lemon quarters, for serving

Scale and clean the anchovies, removing the head and the central spine (with luck your fishmonger may do this for you). Open them up, like a book.

In a processor, blend the garlic, parsley and a little salt with sufficient oil to make a soft paste. Smear some of this paste on the inside of each anchovy fillet, stack them up, cover and leave in the fridge for at least an hour.

Dip each anchovy into the beaten egg, then into the breadcrumbs. Heat the oil to 370°F/188°C and fry the anchovies a few at a time, skin-side up, turning them over as soon as they turn golden-brown underneath.

Remove from the oil with a slotted spoon, blot with kitchen paper and serve straight away, with lemon quarters.

Baked Lettuce Hearts with Anchovy and Tomato Sauce

In Spain, this would usually be made with *cogollos de Tudela*, an exceptionally tender and delicate variety of lettuce from Navarre, often served as a first course salad with a simple oil and anchovy dressing.

SERVES 4 AS A FIRST COURSE

8 lettuce hearts or Little Gem lettuces	250g/9 oz tomatoes, peeled, seeded and chopped
1 flat tin of Cantabrian anchovies	150ml/5 fl oz single cream
1 large garlic clove	1 tablespoon dried breadcrumbs
	Sugar
	Salt

Preheat the oven to 180°C/350°F/Gas Mark 4.

Cut off any thick stalk at the base of the lettuces and tie a loop of string around each lettuce heart – this will help them keep their shape. Blanch in simmering salted water in a covered pan for 5 minutes, then drain and set aside.

Drain the anchovies, reserving the oil. Set aside 4 whole anchovies (i.e. 8 fillets), and pound the remainder with the garlic in a mortar or a food processor. Mix this paste with the tomatoes, cream and a pinch of sugar.

Remove the strings and arrange the lettuce hearts in a heatproof dish. Cover them with the tomato sauce and sprinkle with the breadcrumbs and the reserved anchovy oil. Bake in the preheated oven for 15 minutes. Top each lettuce with an anchovy fillet before serving.

ABOVE: FISHING BOAT, LAREDO
RIGHT: DEEP-FRIED ANCHOVIES WITH GARLIC AND PARSLEY

CASTILE-LA MANCHA:
Manchego lamb and cheese

'The shepherd made Castile great, Castile made
Spain great, and Spain made the world great.'

(Spanish proverb)

counting sheep

The famous sheep of La Mancha have a comic if somewhat ungainly aspect, with protruding jaws, coarse fleece, and large flat ears that stick out horizontally like racing handlebars. Their spindly legs seem unequal to the job, but are sturdy enough to propel these even-tempered beasts great distances in search of fallow pasture and crop stubble. The word Mancha comes from the Arabic *manhsa*, meaning dry land, and in summer the flocks form woolly, spinning circles as they try to stick their heads under each other's stomachs in an attempt to avoid the heat. Queuing in an orderly manner is not a Spanish trait.

In this immense open countryside, dotted with crumbling castles and shuttered, whitewashed villages, where the space and intense summer sun play tricks with the mind and either liberate or suffocate the

senses, Don Quixote confused the sheep with advancing armies, and windmills with giants. Even in early summer, when the golden wheatfields are gashed with blood-red poppies and the wind ruffles the grass like moiré silk, the modern wind turbines that straddle the distant mountains take on the guise of Olympic gymnasts tumbling and turning in formation. Cervantes has a lot to answer for, but although the tourist trail presence of Don Q is inescapable – 'I'll bet,' said Sancho, 'that before long there won't be a wine-shop or a tavern, an inn or a barber's shop, where the history of our exploits won't be painted up' – the sheer scale of the region makes the visions of the Knight of the Sorrowful Countenance surprisingly persuasive.

Cordero manchego is one of the oldest of the Spanish native breeds, long adapted to the tough terrain and extremes of climate: nine months of winter, three months of hell, they say. Sancho's practicality is the

OPPOSITE: (LEFT TO RIGHT) BELMONTE CASTLE; MANCHEGO SHEEP
ABOVE: WINDMILLS, MOTA DEL CUERVO

TOP: COUNTRY HOUSE RECEPTION ROOM, LA DEHESA DE LOS LLANOS. ABOVE LEFT: ELO LÓPEZ COOKING *CALDERETA*

ABOVE RIGHT: HUNTING LODGE LUNCH, LA DEHESA DE LOS LLANOS. OPPOSITE: BAR SIGN, ALMAGRO

counterpoint to Quixote's romantic dreams, and the people of La Mancha are nothing if not down to earth. At La Dehesa de Los Llanos, the 1,000-hectare home of the Marquis of Larios for generations, near the cutlery and knives city of Albacete, head shepherd Eduardo Olivaz told me that he came from generations of shepherds. And yes, he had always wanted to work with animals, but his greatest satisfaction came out of raised production levels. The flock of seven thousand sheep was now reared with all the advantages of modern husbandry, he said proudly. Of course. Leave the romantic notions to foolish foreign food writers.

Nonetheless, there have been sheep here since Palaeolithic times, and the flocks became an integral part of the warring, medieval landscape, providing meat, milk and valuable wool. Mutton was always stewed, and at the beginning of *Don Quixote* Cervantes mentions it as an ingredient of the courtly *caballero*'s casserole, the famous (or infamous) *olla podrida*. Lamb, however, was to become so cheap and abundant that Alexander Dumas wrote in 1846 of a friend who, after eating it for a whole month, 'found himself obliged to leave the country in order to be able to eat something else'.

Suckling lamb was once the preserve of aristocratic tables, and none could have been more delicate or tender than the tiny chops we were served for lunch at La Dehesa's elegantly rustic hunting lodge. Cook Elo Lopez had grilled them over an open fire of Kermes oak and dried rosemary; in the wood-fired Castilian wall oven she roasted juicy legs of baby lamb with garlic and rosemary, using a long-handled paddle to shuffle the dishes with all the skill of a casino card-sharp, so that each cooked evenly in the fierce but falling heat.

'Un cordero sin siesta, no es un buen cordero,' quoted Antonio Martínez Flores, President of the Manchego Lamb Regulatory Council – if you don't need a siesta after eating lamb, then you've not eaten a good one. 'Manchego lamb is the best you can get. We've had to fight to protect ourselves from unfair competition but, bit by bit, Spanish housewives are learning to understand you get what you pay for.' We were fourteen around the table, served by uniformed staff in white gloves, and the mood had slipped from exquisite civility to more casual bonhomie now formalities were over and well-fed tummies strained against over-tight belts.

The estate is centred round a palace and former Franciscan monastery. It is named after the image of the Virgin Mary found on the land in 1285. The present owner, the Marquis of Paúl, runs it to the highest of conservation standards, growing wheat, maize, onions, garlic, potatoes, sugar beet and poppies. He also produces an exceptional Manchego cheese using milk solely from his own flock, like a fine château wine. In the manager's office, I was shown a photograph of endless rows of red-legged partridges laid out on the ground, memory of a great shooting party when a record 8,000 were bagged over two days. The *cordero manchego* breeding book also told its proud tale of agricultural shows and competition winners. But it was hard to keep track: sated with good wine and roast lamb, I was starting to count Manchego sheep. *Claro*, time for a siesta.

NOTE: In place of Manchego, use rare-breed lamb for maximum flavour.

Lamb Cutlets with Fresh Fig Sauce

The best way to grill lamb is over a wood fire fragrant with vine cuttings. In all the wine-growing areas of Spain, after the harvest, simply follow your nose to a good *horno asador* (restaurant with roasting oven) for a plate piled high with baby chops and cutlets. In place of that elusive scent, this sauce uses the fruit of a tree that is as much a part of the Spanish landscape as the vine and the olive.

SERVES 2

Small lamb cutlets or chops
(as many as you think you
can eat)
1 tablespoon oil
8 ripe fresh figs, quartered

1 tablespoon honey
1 tablespoon sherry vinegar
3 tablespoons PX sherry
Salt and black pepper

Grill the chops, and while they are cooking heat the oil over medium heat in a small frying pan. Quickly sauté the figs, and add the honey. Cook for a few minutes, stirring carefully so as not to mash the fruit. Add the vinegar, cook a little longer and pour in the sherry. Season well.

Let the sauce bubble away for 5 minutes until it starts to thicken. Serve hot with the cutlets.

Roast Lamb with Garlic and Parsley

Earthenware dishes of quartered, milk-fed baby lamb, roasted in vaulted, wood-fired ovens with the aid of long paddles as if they were pizzas, have a pale colour, delicate texture and very little fat. The roasting process needs expert judgement, but the result is crisp, golden skin, melting flesh and delicious juices that run down your chin. However, as suckling lamb is not usually found outside Spain, the best substitute is spring lamb, and it is better to use two small joints instead of one large one.

The person who passed on this recipe to me described it as 'finger-licking good, suitable for Christmas, New Year, Easter, and all year round!'

SERVES 4–6

40 g/1½ oz fresh parsley, chopped
4 medium garlic cloves, crushed
About 8 tablespoons olive oil
2 tablespoons lemon juice
2 shoulders or legs of lamb
  on the bone (about 1 kg/
  2 lb 4 oz each)

1 kg/2 lb 4 oz potatoes, peeled,
  washed and thinly sliced
  (optional, or you can
  substitute quarters of
  peeled onion)
50 ml/2 fl oz white wine
Salt and white pepper

Mix together the parsley, garlic, oil and lemon juice and add salt and white pepper. Smear this paste into both sides of the meat and marinate in the fridge for several hours or overnight. Remove from the fridge an hour before roasting, so it comes to room temperature.

Preheat the oven to 230°C/450°F/Gas Mark 8. Arrange the potatoes in a lightly oiled ovenproof dish and place the lamb, skin-side down, on top, together with any remaining marinade. Drizzle with the wine.

Roast for 15 minutes per 500 g for medium lamb (10–12 minutes for rare), and after the first 15 minutes turn the heat down to 180°C/350°F/Gas Mark 4. Baste the lamb from time to time, and turn it over halfway through. Ten minutes before the end, raise the oven temperature to 200°C/400°F/Gas Mark 6 so that the skin turns golden. (Another little *truco* used by some cooks is to drizzle a teaspoon of vinegar over the lamb at the end to help it crisp.)

LEFT: LAMB CUTLETS WITH FRESH FIG SAUCE

Caldereta

Caldereta is a lamb or kid stew, found with many regional variations throughout Spain. It dates from the time shepherds would cross the country from summer to winter pastures with their vast flocks of sheep during the *trashumancia*.

Elo López's original recipe served about 20 people, and was cooked over a wood fire in a huge *sartén con piedras*, a deep sauté pan with three legs.

She used a mixture of shoulder on the bone and chops, hacked ruthlessly into small pieces with a terrifyingly large cleaver.

SERVES 4–6

1 kg/2 lb 4 oz onions, finely
  chopped
Olive oil
1.2 kg/2 lb 12 oz mixture of
  shoulder lamb on the bone
  and chops, chopped into small
  pieces (or use cubed boned
  shoulder lamb)
2–3 bay leaves

400 g/14 oz tinned tomatoes,
  puréed
10 garlic cloves, 6 left unpeeled
  and 4 peeled and crushed
250 ml/9 fl oz white wine
600 ml/20 fl oz water
50 g/1¾ oz almonds, toasted
50 g/1¾ oz lambs' liver
Salt

Heat 3 tablespoons of olive oil in a large casserole and fry the onions very gently for about 30 minutes. Remove from the casserole and set aside.

Heat a little more oil in the casserole, add the lamb, bay leaves and a little salt, and cook very slowly for about 20 minutes. Add the tomatoes and the whole garlic cloves and simmer for a good 15 minutes, stirring frequently.

Add the wine and simmer steadily for about 40 minutes. Add the water and bring to the boil. Keep the heat medium-high and leave the stew to bubble away for a further 20–30 minutes. Stir in the reserved onion. Mix some of the sauce into the crushed garlic, and stir into the stew. Reduce the heat and simmer for 10 minutes.

Pound the almonds in a mortar (you can use a mini-processor but the texture will not be quite right) and set aside. Sprinkle the liver with a little salt. Either grill for a few minutes on each side or fry in a little oil, then pound in a mortar until smooth (again, you can use a processor, but see above). Mix the liver with the almonds, adding a little water if necessary – the consistency should be more purée than paste, as it needs to be thoroughly absorbed into the stew. Add to the stew and simmer for another 10 minutes.

cheese and poetry

'Un nuevo corazón, un hombre nuevo
Ha menester, señor, la anima mia,
Desnúdame de mi, que ser podría ,
Que a tu piedad pagase lo que debo.'

'A new heart, a new man
Lord, you must take away my soul
So that at your mercy
I can pay what I owe.'

'To recite poetry while we make cheese,' cried Encarni Navarro, 'is truly wonderful!' The verse was from the seventeenth-century writer Francisco de Quevedo, who lived in nearby Villanueva de los Infantes in the province of Ciudad Real. Cervantes may dominate much of La Mancha, but this graceful town is also proud of the poet who challenged authority with his satirical attacks and died in jail here for his temerity. 'He was a real *tocacojones* (ball-breaker), not afraid to attack the rich and powerful! These were some of his last thoughts,' she added intensely. 'It is as important to know his writing as it is to know how to make Manchego cheese. It is all part of our culture.'

Encarni is an unusually gifted cheese-maker. Originally trained as a cook, she learnt to make cheese only a few years ago at the suggestion of her husband, who worked on the farm owned for over 250 years by the family of the jovial Horacio Fernández de Silva. She had obviously, though, taken to the business like a Manchego sheep to the plains, studying, reading, experimenting and practising until satisfied she was at least on the right track towards perfection.

A local saying goes that *'Quesos de La Mancha a España ensancha'* – cheese from La Mancha has made Spain famous. Yet, in the most famous book in the Spanish language, this most famous of cheeses gets a pretty poor write-up. In an unfortunate passing reference, Cervantes describes a sample as 'harder than if it had been made out of sand and lime'. That was in 1605, but since then, perhaps on the basis that all publicity is good publicity, Manchego has become the elder statesman of Spanish cheeses. More importantly, the good news is that things have improved out of all recognition.

The milk, however, still comes solely from the Manchego sheep, which can yield milk even on the hottest days of summer, and the rind is still imprinted with the characteristic basket-weave pattern of the mould, originally made from plaited strands of esparto grass. Both pasteurized industrial cheese and hand-made, raw milk versions have to be aged for a minimum of sixty days, and the results can range from

ABOVE: MANCHEGO SHEEP, NEAR VILLANUEVA DE LOS INFANTES.
RIGHT: (LEFT TO RIGHT) ENCARNI NAVARRO IN THE CHEESE AGEING ROOM; *PLEITA Y FLOR* MANCHEGO CHEESE

soft, crumbly and creamy to well-matured and hard-textured, depending on whether the cheese is sold semi-ripened, ripe or aged when it is excellent for grating. At its best, D.O. *Manchego* has an elegant balance of slightly salty, slightly toasty flavours, warm and rich in the mouth. Don Quixote actually offers the best example of how to eat it – simply with bread freshly baked in a wood-fired oven, with a young, fruity red wine. Although it is also a good cooking cheese, it is mostly eaten as *tapas* or, when fairly young, after dinner with *membrillo* (quince paste) or honey. the latter combination is an ancient one: old photographs of La Mancha show itinerant vendors laden with cheese and honey travelling from village to village.

We tasted Encarni's range of cheeses, cut in the traditional triangular wafers with a long, two-handled blade from a wedge of the whole wheel. The ivory-coloured younger cheeses had a fresh clarity of taste; the older ones, with a deeper gold hue, revealed intense, multi-layered complexity. Anyone who dismisses Manchego as predictable should make tracks for Villanueva, where most of the farm's cheese is sold locally, under the *Pleita y Flor* label. Horacio explained there was a natural limit to production. To increase the 1,500 flock would mean compromise, something they were not prepared to do; it was also hard to find shepherds these days. 'The milk from our own sheep is wonderful, but if we bought in milk from other flocks, then we couldn't be so confident about the raw material, we just wouldn't know what they'd been eating.'

Encarni talked me through the process, from the milking ('no one does it by hand any more – that's history!'), through the curdling and curd-cutting, whey removal, moulding, casein-tabbing for identification, pressing, turning, salting, drying and ageing. At every stage she exclaimed, 'Now, this is the most important part of the process!' And it was all true: artisan cheese-making is as much art as skill, a constant interaction of temperature, humidity, technique and intuition. It was hard physical work, cutting and squeezing the curds, then packing them into moulds, yet it all had to be done with a mother's tenderness. Her pride in her 'babies' was palpable and her enthusiasm irrepressible. 'My cheeses vary from day to day, but I am always trying for perfection, the perfect shape, the perfect taste. It is totally absorbing. I look at all the cheeses every day in the ageing room, my kingdom, and think of my mistakes, my successes, my hopes, my dreams… Manchego is known all over the world, but people don't know how it is really made. The more I learn about it, the more enthusiastic I get.'

Stuffed Aubergines with Mushrooms, Pinenuts and Cheese

Baltasar del Alcázar, a sixteenth-century poet from Seville, dedicated a whole poem to his three passions: 'The lovely Inés, ham and aubergines with cheese.'

SERVES 4

4 large aubergines	250 g/9 oz mushrooms, finely
1 onion, finely chopped	sliced
2 tablespoons oil, plus extra for	50 g/1¾ oz pinenuts, lightly
drizzling	toasted
2 garlic cloves, finely chopped	25 g/1 oz fresh parsley, chopped
1 large tomato, skinned, seeded	200 g/7 oz Manchego cheese,
and chopped	grated
½ teaspoon ground cinnamon	Salt and black pepper

Preheat the oven to 180°C/350°F/Gas Mark 4.

Cut the aubergines lengthways and make a few deep slashes over the surface. Arrange, cut-side up, on an ovenproof tray, drizzle with olive oil and bake for 20 minutes, until they are soft and cooked through but still hold their shape. Remove from the oven and set aside, but don't turn the oven off.

While the aubergines are baking, slowly fry the onion in the oil for at least 10 minutes until it becomes soft and golden. Add the garlic, and when the aroma arises, add the tomato. Fry for a minute, then add the cinnamon, salt and pepper. Add the mushrooms and cook for about 5 minutes, until they have released their juices.

As soon as the aubergines are cool enough to handle, scoop out the pulp (a serrated grapefruit knife is useful here), keeping the shells intact. Chop the pulp and stir into the mushroom mixture. Fry for another minute then add the pinenuts and parsley.

Pack the aubergine shells into a lightly oiled baking dish and stuff each with some of the mushroom mixture. Sprinkle with the Manchego cheese and put back in the oven for 5 minutes, until the cheese melts.

LEFT: STUFFED AUBERGINES WITH MUSHROOMS, PINENUTS AND CHEESE.

Manchego Cheese Fritters

The Spanish love deep-fried fritters, doughnuts and pastries of all kinds, and there are as many batters as there are stars in the Castilian sky. This version is based on one in *The Food and Wines of Spain* by Penelope Casas. Use plenty of hot oil for a crisp result.

MAKES ABOUT 20

2 large eggs, separated	1 small onion, grated
125 ml/4 fl oz full fat milk	Salt
75 g/2¾ oz plain flour	Oil for deep-frying
225 g/8 oz mature Manchego	
cheese, grated	

Lightly whisk the egg yolks and stir in the milk and flour. Make sure there are no lumps.

Beat the egg whites with a pinch of salt until they just start to stand in snowy peaks. Fold the egg yolk mixture into the whites, along with the cheese and the onion.

Heat the oil and when it's very hot, drop in rounded tablespoons of the mixture, a few at a time only. The fritters will bob up to the surface; flip them over as soon as the bottom side turns light gold. As soon as the other side is the same colour, remove with a slotted spoon, drain on kitchen paper and serve sprinkled with salt.

Baked Eggs with Tomatoes, Chorizo and Cheese

SERVES 4

2 tablespoons olive oil	8 large eggs
4 large ripe tomatoes, skinned,	8 slices of chorizo
seeded and chopped	50 g/1¾ oz Manchego cheese,
2 tablespoons chopped parsley	grated
Crushed chilli peppers	Salt

Preheat the oven to 180°C/350°F/Gas Mark 4. Heat the oil in a frying pan and slowly cook the tomatoes for 15 minutes until thick. Stir in the parsley and season with crushed chillies and salt.

Divide the tomato sauce between four shallow heatproof dishes and break 2 eggs into each dish. Place a slice of chorizo on each egg and top with grated cheese. Bake in the preheated oven for 10–15 minutes, until the whites are set but the yolks still soft.

CASTILE-LEON:
Morucha beef

angels and cowboys

At the University of Salamanca, the oldest in Spain, eighteenth-century theologians once furiously debated the language of angels. The question still seems pertinent in the perfectly proportioned, enclosed Plaza Mayor, fashioned from butterscotch sandstone. During the evening *paseo*, when the city is young and full of life, the cafés and arcades are packed until an invisible stagehand directs the scholars and shoppers to leave the set. In minutes the square empties, its noble beauty left to the swallows swerving overhead in demented overdrive and the conclave of strangely donnish storks, impassive on their high nests. In this poised, golden city, carved with the fantastic conceits of the Spanish *churrigueresco*, it is easy to believe in angels and devils and mythological beasts with long, curved horns.

The rare-breed Morucha cattle of Salamanca have striking looks, as if they had just stepped out of a prehistoric cave painting. These are not the *gemütlich* Friesians of northern fairy tales, but surely the descendants of the fearsome model for the statue that guards the Roman bridge into the city. The Morucha are held to be the eco-model for other surviving native breeds, and their lineage can be traced back to the *Bos Taurus Ibericus*, one of the earliest branches of the bovine family known to man. The lean, finely grained meat is richly coloured and juicy, with a deep, almost spicy flavour, highlighted in the city's menus in the form of wafer-thin slices of raw carpaccio beef, spicy heaps of steak tartar or as slow-cooked casseroles, entrecôtes and immense rib steaks that come seared and sizzling to the table, almost raw, on hot earthenware platters.

OPPOSITE: MORUCHA CATTLE . ABOVE: STATUE OF FRAY LUIS DE LEÓN, SALAMANCA UNIVERSITY

Over the centuries this robust, muscular breed, originally used as beasts of burden or for bullfighting, has adapted to the sparse Castilian scrubland around Salamanca and is able to withstand burning summers, freezing winters and extreme temperature swings from day to night. The grey and black cattle are extensively reared on the *dehesas*, vast, rocky woodlands quartered by dry-stone walls, dotted with drinking pools. The herds freely graze on pasture, grass, harvest stubble, thistles, acorns and leaves; the Morucha await the annual pruning of the holm and cork oaks with all the anticipation of Tiny Tim for his Christmas dinner, stripping the fallen branches until they are bare as a turkey carcass. They are remarkably agile, and the only way to get close to them is by horse – or four-wheel drive.

'They look peaceful, but you'd better stay in the car. The cows give birth in the fields, and the calves stay with them for up to nine months. They have a strong maternal instinct and get very defensive,' warned Eloy Vaquero Hernández, Technical Director of the Morucha Regulatory Council, cheerfully adding, 'When you want to round them up or move them, you have to carry a long wooden lance to prod them along. I should know, my name is *vaquero* – cowboy!' The day the animals are branded and tagged is eagerly anticipated; it's a good excuse for a party. To stoke up for the job ahead, there are plates of *patatas de herradero*, spicy fried potatoes with salt pork, garlic and onion.

We were on the farm where Eloy had grown up. The fields were green-gold, but in a few weeks they would take on the arid look of high summer; overhead, kites circled like electric fans, seeking easy prey. As we drove through the countryside under the naked light of the high Castilian sky – the original cowboy country – he pointed out farms and fields belonging to brothers, uncles and cousins, the houses built protectively close together. This was his *patria chica*, where cattle-rearing skills are still passed down the generations.

When we stopped at a farmhouse for a snack of home-cured chorizo, the talk was of breeding cycles, insemination, traceability, price levels, in other words the everyday story of country life.

Most Morucha beef is still sold in the immediate area of Salamanca, but the Regulatory Council, along with the real meat producers of other protected breeds such as those of the Ternera Gallega, Carne de Avila and Carne de Retinto, believe a wider band of consumers increasingly value quality over cost. 'Our biggest problem is profitability,' Eloy reflected. 'Morucha is expensive and slow to rear, and we also have to persuade the average Spanish consumer to buy older, dark-red, more highly flavoured meat than they normally do, but it's so much better than the usual tasteless, pallid stuff you get! The Morucha has survived thanks to a group of enthusiastic ranchers, but we still have more work to do. It's not just that they are quite wonderful animals, it's also a question of *patrimonio*, our heritage.'

NOTE: Substitute Morucha with the best rare-breed beef you can find.

ABOVE: CATEDRAL NUEVA, SALAMANCA. RIGHT: (TOP LEFT TO RIGHT, CLOCKWISE) STUDENTS, SALAMANCA; FOOD SHOP, SALAMANCA; *ABUELAS* AFTER CHURCH, SALAMANCA

Marinated Steak with Tomato and Pepper Sauce

In Spain this is often served with a few small fried green peppers, as well as the inevitable mound of chips or fried potatoes.

SERVES 4

4 large rib steaks	1 large onion, finely chopped
5 large garlic cloves, 3 finely chopped and 2 peeled but left whole	1 green pepper, finely chopped
	500 g/1 lb 2 oz tomatoes, skinned, seeded and chopped
Juice of 2 lemons	25 g/1 oz fresh parsley, chopped
100 ml/3½ fl oz olive oil	Salt and black pepper

Marinate the steaks with the chopped garlic, lemon juice, salt and pepper and two-thirds of the oil. Leave in the fridge for an hour. Remove about 10 minutes before cooking, so the meat comes to room temperature.

Heat the remaining oil and gently fry the onion, green pepper and whole garlic cloves for at least 10 minutes until soft.

Add the tomatoes, season and simmer for 30 minutes. Add the parsley. (This sauce can be made in advance, and reheated while the steaks are cooking.)

Grill or fry the steaks, and serve with the sauce. (If you don't like the characteristic, caramelized taste of slightly burnt garlic, wipe off the marinade with kitchen paper before you grill them. Once cooked, you can also sprinkle the steaks with a little sea salt.

Steak with Cabrales Sauce

Another popular way of serving steak is with a sauce made from the star cheese of Asturias, blue Cabrales. For 4 people, melt a nut of butter in a saucepan over a low heat and stir in 100 g/3½ oz of crumbled cheese. When it's almost melted, add 4 tablespoons of single cream. Stir gently until the sauce is smooth, and finish with a little black pepper and a handful of chopped chives.

LEFT: MARINADED STEAK WITH TOMATO AND PEPPER SAUCE
ABOVE: OLD CITY CENTRE, SALAMANCA

Oxtail Stew with Chestnuts

Chestnuts roasting on the brazier signal the start of autumn in Spain, and the scent from trays of hot nuts are irresistible. This is a cold-weather, country stew, made either with tails from the fighting bulls for which Salamanca is also renowned or with oxtail.

SERVES 4

2 kg/4 lb 8 oz oxtail, in pieces	2 sprigs of fresh rosemary (or thyme)
2 tablespoons flour	
2 tablespoons olive oil	400 g/14 oz prepared chestnuts (vacuum-packed whole ones are ideal)
1 large onion, chopped	
2 garlic cloves, chopped	
1 bottle of robust red wine (a good Toro would be apt)	1 teaspoon sugar
	Salt
10 peppercorns	Chopped fresh parsley (optional)

Preheat the oven to 150°C/300°F/Gas Mark 2.

Lightly salt the meat and dust with the flour. Heat the oil in a frying pan and brown the oxtail in batches. Remove the meat from the pan and place in a large lidded casserole.

Fry the onion in the same frying pan, adding more oil if necessary, for about 5 minutes until soft. Add to the oxtail, along with all the remaining ingredients except the parsley. Bring to the boil, skimming off any scum that rises to the surface.

Cover the casserole and bake in the preheated oven for 3–4 hours, until the meat is tender. The stew can be made in advance, and the fat removed from the surface before it is reheated. Serve scattered with parsley, if wished.

Beef with Olives and Almonds

The green olives, nuts and cinnamon show a definite Moorish influence, perhaps more Andalucian than Castilian, but extremely good nonetheless.

SERVES 4

2–3 tablepoons olive oil

1 kg/2 lb 4 oz braising steak, cut into slices about 5 cm/ 2 inches thick and coated with seasoned flour

1 large onion, sliced

1 large garlic clove, finely chopped

2 large tomatoes, peeled, seeded and chopped

1 heaped teaspoon cinnamon

100 g/3½ oz green olives, pitted

100 g/3½ oz almonds, blanched

500 ml/18 fl oz stock

1 glass of red wine

Salt and black pepper

Preheat the oven to 180°C/350°F/Gas Mark 4.

Heat the oil in a lidded casserole and brown the meat on both sides. You may need to do this in batches. Remove and set aside.

Add the onion to the casserole and fry for about 10 minutes until wilted, adding a little more oil if needed. Stir in the garlic, tomatoes and cinnamon, followed by the olives and almonds.

Put the meat back into the dish, add the stock and wine, and season with salt and pepper. Go easy on the former, as the olives will already have added some salt to the sauce. Cover with a lid and cook in the preheated oven for 2 hours, stirring occasionally.

Beef with Red Wine, Prunes and Pinenuts

The consumption of meat in Spain has always been an indicator of social standing. An old expression holds that it is better to have two mouthfuls of beef than seven of potatoes. This sustaining, rich Castilian stew may help you decide.

SERVES 4

4 tablespoons olive oil

1 kg/2 lb 4 oz shin or other casserole beef, cut into large chunks and seasoned with salt and ground black pepper

150 g/5½ oz prunes

A dozen shallots, peeled (or small pickling onions)

3 large carrots, peeled and sliced thickly

500 ml/18 fl oz red wine

50 g/1¾ oz pinenuts, toasted, or chopped parsley

Salt and black pepper

Heat the oil in a lidded casserole over a medium heat, and brown the beef on all sides. Add the rest of the ingredients except for the pinenuts or parsley. Cover and cook over a low heat for 2 hours or until the meat is tender, stirring occasionally.

Leave to stand overnight to deepen the flavour. When reheated, serve sprinkled with toasted pinenuts or parsley.

ABOVE: PLAZA MAYOR, SALAMANCA

RIGHT: BEEF WITH RED WINE, PRUNES AND PINENUTS

CASTILE-MADRID:
Chinchón garlic

'En tiempo nevado, un ajo vale lo que un caballo.'
'In snowy weather, garlic is worth as much as a horse.'
(Spanish proverb)

still life with garlic

For centuries, daily life in the small town of Chinchón, fifty kilometres from Madrid, has revolved around the enchanting Plaza Mayor, enclosed by a perfectly preserved terrace of sixteenth-century houses with a double layer of wooden balconies. The central space feels almost as sealed off from the modern world as the nearby cloistered convent of the Hermanas Clarisas, renowned for its almond biscuits, which are sold through a revolving wooden turntable set in the wall like a portal to a sweet hereafter.

Getting a ringside table at one of the square's famous *mesones* on summer weekends is nigh impossible; Orson Welles is not the only one to have fallen under its spell. The sense of drama derives not just from the theatrical curve of the buildings, but also from the knowledge that many of the defining events of

Castilian history have been played out on this public stage: markets, fairs, tournaments, plays, religious processions, political proclamations, military round-ups and executions. The town's famous Easter passion play is still enacted here by local residents; in summer it is transformed into the world's most beautiful bullring. They say bullfighters carry a clove of garlic to keep them from harm, but although the town is as famous for garlic as it is for anís, oil and wine, it is the *ajo fino de Chinchón* that is in need of protection.

Early one Sunday, as the sloping, slightly irregular *plaza* was flooded with sunlight so bright it pained the eyes and the stallholder selling cheap sunglasses was looking forward to a good day's business, another vendor was also setting out his wares. The garlic-seller had strung up traditional plaits and was arranging bags of loose, plump bulbs. '*Ajo fino?*' I asked. He shook his head. 'No, *ajo blanco*, white garlic.

OPPOSITE: GARLIC ON SALE, CHINCHÓN. ABOVE: GARLIC FIELDS NEAR CHINCHÓN

'Do not eat garlic and onions, for their smell will reveal you are a peasant.' Don Quixote to Sancho

They're still from Chinchón, very good quality, but *ajo fino* is hard to find these days. I had some two weeks ago, grown by a friend, but the season is short, the cost high and the supply unpredictable. Everyone wants *ajo blanco* these days, even though the taste is not the same.'

Ajo fino may have been grown in the Chinchón area since the eighteenth century, according to documents in the Municipal Archive. This special, local variety of garlic has a pink tinge and an intense, spicy taste and aroma: the bulb and elongated cloves are small and even, but a little goes a long way. Today, however, as Alicia Zacarias, third-generation member of one of the town's main packing, wholesale and export companies, explained, 'Many people, especially in northern Europe, want the bulbs to look big and beautiful, fat and white, even if they taste bland, so *ajo blanco* is our main crop. The Spanish like the purple *morado* garlic that comes from Las Pedroneras, Córdoba and elsewhere in La Mancha – even from here! It's more *picante*, more like the original *ajo fino*, but easier to grow.'

It was all a bit confusing, but I was getting the message. Garlic was an important part of the town's economy, but it was a modern business, facing the practicalities and demands of modern commerce. And there was little place for sentimentality about old varieties. Success is measured in Mercedes, not memories. It was different in Alicia's grandfather's day. 'He had a few fields where he grew garlic, as well as beans, potatoes and sugar beet. When my father married, he decided to try to sell produce to the Madrid markets, and our company grew from there.'

The main harvest takes place in June and July, hand-pulled from the fertile Vega pastures that follow the course of the Tajuña and Jarama rivers. As the bulbs dry in the baking Castilian sun for ten to twelve days, a penetrating scent drifts through the back streets of the town – although a modern hot-air dryer is now kept as back-up, since rain can blight the crop. The garlic is then hand-trimmed and cleaned, graded, weighed, packed and kept in chilled storage for staggered release throughout the year. Old-fashioned 'pigtails' are said to be one of the best ways to lock in flavour and aroma, but only a few bother to braid the bulbs any more. 'There's really no market for it other than for tourists,' explained Alicia. 'It looks picturesque, but it's too expensive to do on a large scale.'

The garlic industry was also facing other problems. 'It is increasingly difficult to earn decent money; costs get higher and the supermarkets pay ever lower prices. Some families have given up and it's harder to find people to work in the fields. Production levels have not fallen, but farming is far more mechanized. The government should give us more help to keep the *ajo fino*, it would be very sad if it died out.'

Once upon a time, garlic was the spice of the rural poor; in the fourteenth century, King Alfonso of Castile forbade any knight smelling of garlic to enter his palace. Those days may be long past, with every Spaniard eating on average over 1.5 kilos of the bulb each year, but then Alicia added, like a true Spanish princess, 'Personally, I don't like eating anything with garlic in it at all! I simply hate the smell.'

ABOVE: CYCLISTS, CHINCHÓN. RIGHT: (TOP LEFT TO BOTTOM RIGHT) SUNGLASSES STALL, PLAZA MAYOR, CHINCHÓN; *FLORES* (LOCAL PASTRIES), CHINCHÓN; PLAZA MAYOR, CHINCHON

Roast Pepper, Tomato and Garlic Salad

This salad from Extremadura is found in various permutations throughout Spain. It is based on a recipe from the excellent *Gourmetour* magazine, published by the Spanish Institute for Foreign Trade.

SERVES 4

500 g/1 lb 2 oz large, ripe tomatoes

1 kg/2 lb 4 oz mixed peppers

1 whole, unpeeled head of garlic

4 tablespoons olive oil

1 tablespoon sherry vinegar

Salt

2 hard-boiled eggs, quartered (optional)

Preheat the oven to 200°C/400°F/Gas Mark 6.

Cut a small cross on the top of each tomato and place them in a large roasting pan or on a baking sheet, along with the whole peppers and the head of garlic. (The cross will help prevent the tomato from bursting as it roasts and will make peeling easier.) Rub all the vegetables with olive oil and roast in the preheated oven for 30–40 minutes.

Remove from the oven; cover the dish with a cloth and leave to cool for at least an hour. Peel off the papery covering of the roast garlic and press out as much of the soft garlic paste as you can into the bottom of a serving dish, as if squeezing the last of the toothpaste. (This is a bit of a messy job, but do the best you can.) Peel the tomatoes and peppers, cut into pieces and add to the dish. Dress with the oil, vinegar and salt and combine well.

This keeps well for several days, but is best served at room temperature, topped, if wished, with quarters of hard-boiled egg.

Garlic Soup

Many recipes in Spain include bread either as base or extra ingredient; cheap and nourishing, virtually every restaurant, indeed every home, in Spain has its own version of this comforting, rustic garlic soup that only *mamita* makes best. Although usually made with water, chicken stock raises this from a poor man's dish to one fit for a *mesa burguesa*. It is also recommended as a hangover cure.

PER PERSON:

3 tablespoons olive oil

3 garlic cloves, peeled and lightly crushed

1 thick slice of sourdough or country bread

1 teaspoon *pimentón de la Vera*

500 ml/18 fl oz chicken stock

1 egg

Salt

Heat the oil and lightly fry the garlic so that the oil absorbs the flavour. When the garlic starts to darken, remove from the pan and discard. Fry the bread in the same oil, then tear into pieces and place in the bottom of an earthenware bowl.

Add the *pimentón* to the oil and fry for a few seconds only – it must not burn – before adding the stock. Bring to the boil and simmer for 10 minutes. At this point either:

1. Beat the egg and stir into the broth until just set. Pour over the bread in the bowl.

2. Poach the egg in the broth, then ladle both over the bread.

3. Break an egg over the bread, pour over the hot broth and place in a hot oven for a few minutes until the egg is poached.

ABOVE: BULLFIGHTERS' BAR, CHINCHÓN

RIGHT: ROAST PEPPER, TOMATO AND GARLIC SALAD

Garlic and Chilli Prawns

A popular-going-on-ubiquitous tapas dish, found throughout Spain.

SERVES 4–6

6 tablespoons olive oil
500 g/1 lb 2 oz peeled raw
  prawns
3 garlic cloves, finely chopped

Crushed chillies, from a mill, or
  finely diced dried or fresh red
  chillies, as preferred
Salt

Heat the oil in a flameproof earthenware dish over a medium-high heat. As soon as the oil starts to shimmer, throw in the prawns, garlic and chillies. Fry vigorously for a few minutes, then add salt and serve, still sizzling, in the dish (the prawns will carry on cooking as you take them to the table).

Muledrivers' Salt Cod

Bacalao ajoarriero takes its name from the time when shepherds and muleteers travelled throughout the country and would stop to eat dishes such as this in the equivalent of today's truck-stops. Salt cod is still enormously popular in Spain, a leftover from the times when abstinence from meat (and other pleasures of the flesh) was demanded by the Church. It needs to be soaked in cold water for 24–36 hours, with two or three changes of water, then drained and rinsed. If good-quality salt cod (look for a grey, rather than a yellowish colour) is unobtainable, this dish can be made using fresh. Keep all the chopped vegetables equal in size.

SERVES 4

4 tablespoons olive oil
500 g/1 lb 2 oz ripe tomatoes,
  skinned and chopped
1 large onion, chopped
1 whole hot dried chilli pepper
4 red peppers, roasted, peeled,
  seeded and chopped
200 g/7 oz potatoes, peeled and
  cubed

1 green pepper, seeded and
  chopped (not roasted)
4 garlic cloves, finely chopped
500 g/1 lb 2 oz salt cod, soaked,
  lightly pre-cooked and flaked
1 teaspoon *pimentón de la Vera*
Salt
25 g/1 oz fresh parsley, chopped

Heat half the oil in a heatproof serving dish and gently fry the tomatoes and onion with the whole chilli for about 10 minutes, until soft. Take off the heat and add the roasted red peppers. Set aside.

Heat the remaining oil in a frying pan and fry the potatoes and green pepper over a medium-high heat until the potatoes are cooked and golden. Add half the garlic and take the pan off the heat once the aroma starts to rise. Lift out the potatoes and peppers with a slotted spoon and add them to the tomato mixture.

In the same frying pan, sauté the salt cod for a few minutes, adding the remaining garlic at the end. Once the garlic is golden, take the pan off the heat and stir in the *pimentón*. Add the fish to the vegetable mixture and cook over a medium-low heat for a few minutes more, stirring gently but frequently. Add salt as necessary, and sprinkle with parsley before serving.

Spicy Monkfish with Saffron and Chillies

This recipe originates in Melilla, an autonomous Spanish city on the northern coast of Morocco. Part of Spain since 1497, it claims the most beautiful (and only active) bullring in Africa, and the best and cheapest seafood in the world! Unusually, this dish contains no onions, but uses plenty of garlic for flavour instead.

SERVES 4

2 tablespoons olive oil
1 head of garlic, the cloves
  finely chopped
2 teaspoons ground cumin
25 g/1 oz fresh parsley, chopped
2 green peppers, seeded and cut
  into strips
1 kg/2 lb 4 oz ripe tomatoes,
  peeled, seeded and chopped

1 teaspoon saffron filaments,
  lightly crushed and soaked in
  a little hot water
2 whole dried chillies
1 kg/2 lb 4 oz monkfish fillet, cut
  into pieces
50 g/1¾ oz cooked peas
Salt and ground black pepper

Heat the oil in a pan over a medium heat and fry the garlic until it starts to colour. Add the cumin, then the parsley, and fry until the parsley wilts. Add the peppers and cook until they start to soften, then add the tomatoes. Lower the heat, and simmer for 10 minutes.

Add the saffron, chillies, salt and black pepper, and continue to simmer for 20 minutes. (If you like, you can remove the chillies at this stage and purée the sauce in a blender, adding a little water or fish stock as necessary.)

Add the monkfish and poach for about 5 minutes, until the fish is cooked. Finally add the peas, and serve as soon as they are hot. (Don't forget to fish out the chillies if they are still in the sauce.)

CATALONIA: Reus hazelnuts

Señor Avellana

'Do you want to buy the farm?' In the pale, winter sunlight the rows of hazelnut trees, pruned in the classic vase shape, seemed a desirable asset, not one to casually peddle to a passing stranger. The trees were heavy with bleached catkins the texture of chenille, flapping in the wind as if they were Buddhist prayer rags. The farmhouse was smart and modern, the driveway flanked by roses, the acid flash of mimosa and rotund palms like sprouting pineapples. On the horizon, the city of Reus looked flat and fragile.

José Blanqué Corral had come from Granada over forty years ago, during the notorious *años de hambre* (years of hunger). He and his Catalan wife, Consuelo, had worked hard to build a fine farm with

over 3,000 trees. Now, however, his sons work in Madrid and Barcelona; they love the land but it's not their future any more. More to the point, hazelnuts are not the profitable crop they used to be. The issue hung like a small, dark cloud in the clear Catalan sky.

Reus is famous for *avellanas* or hazelnuts, although the city's original fortunes were founded on wine. Once, Reus was not just the second city in Catalonia, but a corner of a great trading triangle with London and Paris. Those golden days are reflected in the beautifully restored Fortuny Opera House, dedicated to the memory of one of the city's most famous sons, the *modernista* town houses, and El Círcol, the private dining club founded in 1852, where the city's professional and mercantile élite play cards and discreetly lunch on salt cod salad, hake with garlic sauce, and hazelnut ice cream.

OPPOSITE: (LEFT TO RIGHT) CATKINS ON HAZELNUT TREES, REUS; ROASTED HAZELNUTS

ABOVE: SEÑOR ANTONI BORRÀS, BORGES, NEAR REUS

I had been taken there by Señor Antoni Borràs, otherwise known as 'Señor Reus', 'Señor Avellana' or simply, with a magnificent flourish, as 'Borràs of Reus'. A hazelnut exporter, he was born in 1929 in Borges, a village near Reus, where his grandfather farmed hazelnuts and his father traded them. If anyone is a walking advertisement for the health-giving, efficacious properties of hazelnuts, then it is Señor Borràs. Sprightly, alert, the proud father of seven and grandfather of eleven, he is clearly one of the leading citizens of the town. We do not walk more than a few steps without someone respectfully stopping to shake his hand, ask after the family or exchange some gossip. As we proceed at a stately pace around the prosperous centre, Señor Borràs tells me the story of the rise – and possible fall – of the Reus hazelnut. Cultivated in Catalonia since the twelfth century, the trade was controlled by the Barcelona Commodity Exchange in the thirteenth century. Nonetheless, hazelnut production only began to develop on a significant scale six hundred years later, after *phylloxera* destroyed the wine industry. Since then, Spain has become the fourth largest producer of hazelnuts in the world.

The main variety grown is Negret; although the name comes from the Catalan for 'little black', they are the colour of cinnamon. Their fine flavour, plump shape and easy peeling and roasting properties make them sought after by the chocolate and confectionery industry, although Señor Borràs reflected that in the past they were little used in cooking. 'They were just eaten roasted, with a drink. You'd just put out a dish any time anyone came to the house. But in the last twenty-five years, we have tried to show they are both healthy to eat and good to cook with.'

From the end of August, when the nuts start to fall, the farmers have to act fast. They are swept into piles, then either hand-raked or vacuumed from the ground before they are taken to small factories to be shelled, graded, peeled, dried, processed and roasted as required. 'Twenty years ago,' said Señor Borràs, 'the harvest was poor, but now we have improved cultivation techniques and irrigation.' Unfortunately, twenty years ago even a small harvest brought high prices; now that production has risen, prices have fallen because of fierce international competition. As a result, many trees have been replaced by new groves of Arbequina olive trees, and there are also experimental walnut and pistachio plantations.

Back at the farm, it seemed likely the land would eventually be sold to the petrochemical industry that was creeping across the plain between the mountains and the sea. Señora Corral chimed in. 'What can we do? It's getting harder to make a good living. When we sell, that will be it. The end.'

Well, not if a certain distinguished *caballero* has anything to do with it. It may be the end of one chapter, but it's far from the end of the story, if only for the very good reason that in Señor Antoni Borràs, the hazelnuts of Reus could have no better champion. *¡Viva las avellanas!*

NOTE: Use hazelnuts other than those from Reus, if you really must, but you will have to answer to Señor Borràs for your actions. I disclaim responsibility.

ABOVE: IÑIGO VARGAS INSPECTING THE HAZELNUT TREES IN WINTER. OPPOSITE: REUS CITY CENTRE

Sole with Hazelnut Crust

Mariona Quadrada, cookbook author, cookery teacher and Catalan food expert, gave me this simple, but elegant recipe. It can be made with whole Dover sole (skinned on both sides), whole lemon sole (dark skin removed) or sole and other white fish fillets. The key is not to overcook the fish.

SERVES 4

4 whole sole on the bone or 8 fillets

100 g/3½ fl oz butter, plus a little extra

100 ml/3½ fl oz white wine

100 g/3½ oz lightly toasted Reus hazelnuts, roughly crushed in a mortar

Salt and white pepper

Preheat the oven to 200°C/400°F/Gas Mark 6.

Put the sole in a lightly buttered dish and season with salt and white pepper. Dot with half the butter, pour over the wine and bake in the preheated oven for about 15 minutes (or 10 minutes if filleted). The fish should not be overcooked.

Remove the fish from the oven, sprinkle with a thick layer of nuts and dot with the remaining butter. Return the dish to the oven and bake for a further 2 minutes.

Catalan Squid, Clam and Potato Stew

This lengthy way of cooking squid gives surprisingly tender results. *Picada* is a crushed Catalan paste, typically added halfway through or towards the end of cooking to give texture and complexity of flavour. *Vino rancio* is a fortified wine.

SERVES 6

300 g/10½ oz onions, sliced

Olive oil

500 g/1 lb 2 oz ripe tomatoes, peeled, seeded and chopped

1 litre/1¾ pints fish stock

1 kg/2 lb 4 oz squid, cleaned and sliced

500 g/1 lb 2 oz potatoes, peeled and cut into chunks

1 small slice of country or sourdough bread, without the crust

25 g/1 oz Marcona almonds

25 g/1 oz Reus hazelnuts

2 garlic cloves

1 small pinch of saffron, lightly crushed and soaked in a little hot water

25 g/1 oz fresh parsley, chopped

100 ml/3½ fl oz *vino rancio* (or Amontillado sherry)

500 g/1lb 2 oz clams, scrubbed

Salt

Slowly fry the onions in a large, deep pan, in 2–3 tablespoons of oil, for at least 10 minutes or until they soften and start to turn gold. Add the tomatoes and cook for 5 minutes more. Add the stock and bring to the boil.

Heat a little more oil in a frying pan and quickly fry the squid until just coloured. Add to the stock along with the potatoes and salt to taste. Cover and simmer gently for 2 hours.

Fry the bread in hot olive oil until light brown on both sides, then remove from the pan and set aside. Turn down the heat and fry the nuts for a few seconds until toasted. Remove from the pan and set aside.

Pound the bread, nuts, garlic, saffron and half the parsley in a mortar to make the *picada* (this produces a more pulverized texture than a processor – the aim is to get a paste with as little gritty texture as possible). Stir in the wine and set aside.

Ten minutes before the stew is due to be ready, stir in the *picada*. Five minutes later, add the clams and cook until the shells open. (The Spanish way is to keep the clams in the shell; if preferred, steam, shuck and chuck into the pan at the end.)

Let the stew rest for 5 minutes off the heat, then serve, sprinkled with the remaining chopped parsley.

LEFT: SOLE WITH HAZELNUT CRUST

Candied Cinnamon Hazelnuts

Another recipe from Mariona Quadrada, these sweet, crunchy nuts are usually made with almonds, and are sold by street vendors at all fiestas. Hazelnuts make an excellent alternative.

75 g/2¾ oz granulated sugar
1 teaspoon ground cinnamon
2 teaspoons water

100 g/3½ oz Reus hazelnuts,
   lightly toasted

Put the sugar, cinnamon and water into a frying pan and stir over a medium-high heat until the sugar melts.

Working quickly, stir in the nuts, making sure they are all coated with the sugar before it starts to caramelize and burn.

Turn the nuts out on to a foil-lined baking tray to cool. Use a wooden spoon or your hands (take care not to burn your fingers) to separate the nuts before the sugar coating hardens.

Hazelnut Ice Cream with Hot Chocolate Sauce

Spanish nuns in Mexico were the first to add sugar to cocoa, and at one time the beans were considered so valuable it was forbidden to export them from Spain to other European countries. Eventually in the seventeenth century chocolate was introduced to the French court through the marriages of both Anne of Austria and Princess Maria Teresa. The rest is chocolate history.

SERVES 8

200 g/7 oz Reus hazelnuts,
   toasted
150 g/12 oz Málaga raisins
   (or ones as plump as you
   can find), soaked for several
   hours in a little sherry
500 ml/1 pint double cream
100 g/3½ oz golden or unrefined
   caster sugar

3 large eggs
200 g/7 oz bitter chocolate,
   broken into pieces
200 ml/7 fl oz water
100 g/3½ oz unsalted butter,
   cut into small pieces

Finely chop the hazelnuts and combine with the drained raisins. Whisk the eggs and sugar for about 10 minutes until pale and trebled in volume. Whip the cream until fairly thick, but not stiff, and fold in the nuts and raisins. Gently fold the cream into the egg mixture.

Pour half the mixture into a 2 litre/3½ pint metal mould and freeze for half an hour or until the mixture starts to harden, keeping the other half of the mixture in the fridge.

Remove the semi-frozen ice from the freezer and pour the rest of the mixture over – this helps to keep the fruit and nuts well distributed. Put back in the freezer, and remove about 20 minutes before serving. Turn out of the mould on to a serving dish – it helps if you dip the mould into a bowl of hot water first.

While the ice cream softens sufficiently to cut without breaking the knife, make the chocolate sauce by gently melting the chocolate and water, stirring until smooth. Remove from the heat and slowly stir in the butter until the sauce is glossy. Serve with the ice cream.

ABOVE: *MODERNISTA* HOUSE, REUS
RIGHT: HAZELNUT ICE CREAM WITH HOT CHOCOLATE SAUCE

EXTREMADURA:

pimentón de la Vera

red gold

In autumn, the aroma of smoked peppers drifts through the peaceful fields of the valley of La Vera in northern Extremadura, where medieval stone, wood and adobe villages with melodic names are cooled by runnels of fresh water that tumble down the centre of the narrow streets. A few weeks later, almost tangible clouds of rust-red dust seep from the small mills where the cured peppers are ground into *pimentón*. On the days they grind the *picante*, the strongest variety, the locals probably enjoy the sight of passers-by straining for breath, eyes streaming and white shirts impregnated with traces of 'red gold', the spice on which the fortunes of this paradisiacal valley have depended for centuries.

Like Emperor Charles V, I had taken the heart-pounding high road from the Jerte Valley across the Sierra de Gredos, passing crystal streams of melted snow, granite gorges, Roman bridges and natural swimming pools. It was cherry season, and my route was marked by a trail of stones from the box of luscious *picota* cherries for which Jerte is famous. Charles, too, decided to take it as the crow flies, in order to avoid the longer road via Plasencia, where the mountains crumble into the great plains of Extremadura. Travelling from Flanders in 1556, he was in a hurry to reach his new home at the remote monastery of Yuste, but the most powerful man in the world blithely disregarded the fact that there was barely a track over the mountains and had to be carried in an uncomfortable and undignified fashion by peasants as they hacked their way through woods and undergrowth. When they reached the head of the pass, almost 1,500 metres high, he was said to have declared: 'I will not cross any pass again but that of death itself.' Sadly prophetic, he was only to have eighteen months to enjoy his rural bliss before dying from agonizing gout.

It was partly the quest for spices that motivated Spain's explorers, many of whom came from Extremadura. After Columbus presented Ferdinand and Isabella with the pepper plant at the monastery of Guadalupe, the Hieronymite monks developed the art of drying and grinding the fruit into a spicy powder. It soon became the chosen spice of the poor, lifting meagre rations with its colour and fire.

Shielded by the mountains, the valley of La Vera has a microclimate that particularly favours pepper production. When the rest of central and southern Spain looks yellow, La Vera keeps its many shades of green thanks to a relatively mild climate, good rainfall, pure river water and fertile soil. There are groves of cherry, chestnut, olive, fig, orange and oak trees, as well as fruit and vegetable gardens in the small farms beside the Tiétar river. Tobacco, also, has been grown here ever since it too was introduced from the New World. The distinctive brick warehouses in which the plant is dried dot the landscape, but the future is unsure as European subsidies for tobacco come to an end. On my visit, the farmers were aware they had tough decisions to make, but were reluctant to plant more peppers until sure of demand.

It was also a question of profitability. The production of *pimentón* is a long, skilled and costly one, shared between farmer and miller. Cultivation starts in March when the seeds, saved from the previous

OPPOSITE: (LEFT TO RIGHT) ROMAN BRIDGE OVER THE TIÉTAR RIVER; OFFICIAL LOGO, REGULATORY COUNCIL; PLOUGHING THE FIELDS NEAR JARAÍZ DE LA VERA. ABOVE: ENTRANCE TO PEPPER SMOKING SHED.

year's crop, are planted in beds, to be transplanted to the fields in May. Carefully tended and slowly ripened through the summer, the bright red peppers are harvested by hand between September and November. Three sub-species of *Capsicum annuum* are cultivated, to give the three types of *pimentón*: sweet (*dulce*), bittersweet (*agridulce*) and spicy (*picante*).

Once collected, the peppers are smoked in small sheds or *secaderos*, a labour-intensive process that evolved to stop the peppers from spoiling in the autumnal rains, but which gives the *pimentón* its pungent, oddly addictive character. Piled high on slatted ceilings made from chestnut or alder, which are constructed at a precise level above the smouldering oakwood fires, the smoking takes 10–15 days. The peppers must be patiently turned daily by hand, at just the right moment so that they are dried rather than cooked. Farmers will often sleep by the fire – if they feel cold, they know the fire needs stoking.

The peppers are taken to the mills, where the stalks and some of the seeds are removed. They are slowly stone-ground up to seven times, at a constant temperature in order not to impair the colour or complex, subtle flavour. Filtered until fine as flour, the luminous red powder is packed into tins charmingly decorated with flowers, saints or handsome heroes. Hardworking, warm and hospitable, the people of La Vera season everything they eat with a pinch of spice. In more ways than one, *pimentón* is in their blood.

NOTE: Only buy tins bearing the D.O. label to guarantee the *pimentón* is produced, prepared and packed in La Vera. Just use a pinch until you are used to the flavour, then gradually increase the amount until you find the variety and quantity that suits you best. Although they produce three varieties, most locals only use *agridulce*, adding it to their cooking, as they would salt.

ABOVE: (LEFT TO RIGHT) RESTAURANT SIGN, VALVERDE DE LA VERA; VILLANUEVA DE LA VERA. RIGHT: (TOP TO BOTTOM) WOOD FOR SMOKING PEPPERS, JARAÍZ DE LA VERA; VALVERDE DE LA VERA; MARÍA JOSÉ SANCHEZ CRUZ MAKING *MIGAS*

Wild Mushroom *Tortilla*

The size of the pan is important: *tortilla* (Spanish omelette) needs to look like a thick cake. The outside should be firm but not leathery, golden brown but not burnt, and the inside still a little juicy. The ideal pan should be inherited from your grandmother, fairly deep with a long handle, wiped clean and seasoned with a film of oil, but a fairly lightweight, modern non-stick pan does the job just as well.

One of the best and most inexpensive souvenirs to bring back from Spanish hardware shops is a collection of flat metal pan lids of varying sizes, specially designed for *tortilla*-turning.

SERVES 4

225 g/8 oz ceps or other wild
   mushrooms
50 ml/2 fl oz olive oil
1 tablespoon *pimentón de la Vera*
6 large eggs, lightly beaten with
   a pinch of salt
Salt

TO GARNISH (OPTIONAL)
100 g/3½ oz ceps or other wild
   mushrooms
2 tablespoons olive oil

Fry the mushrooms in the oil over medium-high heat in a non-stick frying pan (20 cm/8 inches diameter across the top). As they start to wilt, turn down the heat. Once soft, add salt and sprinkle in the *pimentón*. Give a quick stir to make sure the mushrooms are evenly coloured, and take off the heat. Remove the mushrooms with a slotted spoon, cool slightly and add to the eggs.

Pour off any remaining oil in the pan, leaving just enough to cover the bottom, and reheat. When the oil has just reached smoking point, pour in the egg and mushroom mixture and lower the heat.

Cook for about 15 minutes until the bottom is set and there is only a small amount of liquid left on the surface (you can place a lid over the pan to help things along). Gently shake the pan from time to time to make sure the *tortilla* does not stick, or use a palette knife to loosen the sides.

Place a large plate over the pan, and – with steady hands and nerve – quickly turn both upside down so the *tortilla* drops on to the plate. Slide it back into the pan and cook briefly until set on the other side. Remove from the heat, but leave the *tortilla* in the pan to 'settle' for a few more minutes. Sauté the garnish mushrooms in the oil, if using, and scatter over the top.

LEFT: WILD MUSHROOM *TORTILLA*

'Rabbit' and Potatoes in the Mountains

The joke – if you hadn't already guessed – is that when the diner asks, 'Where's the rabbit?' the answer is, 'In the mountains.' Although this version comes from Salamanca, it is from a family of cheap and unpretentious potato dishes found throughout Spain. You can use just one variety of *pimentón*, but I like the different layers of flavour both bring to the dish. However, in La Vera they would only use one (*agridulce*), and were perfectly scandalized at the thought of mixing *dulce* and *picante*!

SERVES 2–3

500 g/1 lb 2 oz floury potatoes,
   peeled and cut into chunks
2–3 tablespoons olive oil
1 medium onion, finely chopped
2 whole garlic cloves

2 sprigs of fresh rosemary
2 teaspoons each *pimentón de la
   Vera, dulce* and *picante*
Fresh parsley, chopped
Salt

Parboil the potatoes in salted water. Drain and set aside.

Heat the olive oil in a heatproof dish (or you can use a frying pan) and gently fry the onion over a low heat for at least 10 minutes, until transparent. Add the garlic, and when it starts to colour turn the heat up to medium and add the potatoes. Keep gently stirring and turning them over until they turn brown at the edges. Add more olive oil, if necessary.

Add the rosemary, season with salt, and finally stir in the two kinds of *pimentón*.

Add enough boiling water to come halfway up the side of the dish, carefully stir again, and leave to simmer for 30–40 minutes or until the liquid has reduced to a fairly thick sauce. Sprinkle with parsley before serving.

Migas de la Vera

Migas are fried breadcrumbs usually mixed with bacon, ham, sausages or eggs. There are many variations of this comforting, rustic dish, but María José Sánchez Cruz of Jaraíz de la Vera showed me this local version. She demonstrated how it was traditionally cooked at harvest time over a wood fire at her farm, in a large cauldron blackened from years of use, but it can also be made in a large pot or frying pan on top of the stove.

SERVES 10–12

Olive oil

2.5 kg/5 lb potatoes, peeled and finely sliced

4 dried chilli peppers, cut into pieces (with or without seeds)

6 garlic cloves, finely chopped

400 g/14 oz *panceta* or bacon, diced

2 large tablespoons *pimentón de la Vera*

2 glasses water

2 large loaves of country bread, 3–4 days old, cut into small cubes, roughly 1 kg/2 lb 4 oz

Salt

Heat plenty of olive oil until hazy, and sauté the potatoes over a high heat. When they start to brown, add half the chilli peppers and a sprinkling of salt. Turn the potatoes regularly as they fry, breaking them up roughly with the back of a spoon or a spatula. When crisp and cooked, set the pan aside. (This step can be done in advance).

Heat a little more oil in a large pan. Add the garlic (which Maria slices directly into the pan), and fry over medium heat for a few minutes. When the aroma rises, add the *panceta* or bacon and fry until it browns. Add the remaining peppers, the potatoes and any oil from the pan in which they have been standing.

When the potatoes have warmed through, turn the heat to low and sprinkle in the *pimentón*. Stir quickly for a minute, then add half the water: 'Don't put it all in at once, in case it doesn't need it.' Add the bread, turn the heat up to medium-high, and cook, stirring to stop the cubes clinging together in clumps, until they crisp nicely around the edges and turn the colour of autumn leaves.

All the oil should be absorbed, leaving the bottom of the pan clean, 'but take care not to burn the *migas*, either! If you think they are too hard, pour some more water over the back of a large spoon placed in the centre of the pan, so it just trickles down into the bread cubes. If you think they're too soft, add some extra bread. It's all a matter of instinct – you have to correct as you go along.'

Spicy Fish Fingers

These spicy fish fingers are distantly based on the famous Seville tapas dish *soldaditos de Pavia*, salt cod 'soldiers', and are particularly good served with garlic mayonnaise.

SERVES 4

600 g/1 lb 4 oz fillets of thick white fish, cut into thick strips

100 ml/3½ oz white wine

2 garlic cloves, finely chopped

1 tablespoon fresh parsley, finely chopped

2 teaspoons *pimentón de la Vera, dulce*

Flour and beaten egg, for coating

Olive oil, for deep-frying

Salt and white pepper

Marinate the fish with the wine, garlic, parsley, *pimentón*, salt and pepper for several hours.

Drain (allowing some of the marinade ingredients to cling to the fish), then flour and egg each piece. Deep-fry in hot oil (180°C/350°F) until light gold on each side. Drain on kitchen paper, and serve straight away.

ABOVE: FACTORY SIGN, LA VERA

RIGHT: SPICY FISH FINGERS

GALICIA: mussels

the Virgin of the Carmen

Three solemn drumbeats, and a trembling Virgin rose hesitantly into the air. Swaying gently, with drowning sailors clinging in supplication to the rocks at her feet, she looked down from a rowing-boat awash with primrose carnations and lemon lilies. Literally setting sail on a sea of flowers, supported by a raft of willing young shoulders, she left the granite parish church for her annual journey to the *ría*, one of the great estuaries of the Galician coast, where the fishing families of O Grove would pray for her protection in the year ahead.

Every 16 July, on the *Fiesta del Carmen*, the statue of the Virgin is taken to the main square, accompanied by girls in traditional dress holding cordons of fishing nets; the parade includes dignitaries,

priests and bishops, brass bands, Galician pipers, the sick and disabled, and barefoot pensioners clutching tall candles topped with inverted cups to catch the dripping wax. It is the most important day of the year: this part of Galicia depends heavily on fishing, as well as on holiday tourism, and the memories of natural and man-made disaster are reflected in the public Mass that concludes with the bitter-sweet refrains of the *Salve Marinera*.

With military precision and much heaving, the Virgin then proceeded to the waterfront, where she and her rowing-boat were, improbably, loaded into the prow of a large trawler packed with celebrants. The band played, a jollier, finger-snapping refrain this time, and we set sail escorted by a flotilla of small craft, their passengers applauding the majestic progress of the Virgin as she steamed

OPPOSITE: (LEFT TO RIGHT) LOLI BARREIRO; FRESHLY COOKED MUSSELS; MUSSEL BOAT, O GROVE.

ABOVE: *FIESTA DEL CARMEN*, O GROVE

smartly along. At the point where the estuary met the sea, we stopped; prayers were said and the flowers were thrown into the water. The pipers and drummers tore into their curious hypnotic rhythms, the ships horns boomed and bottles of chilled Albariño wine appeared along with slices of *empanada* stuffed with fat orange mussels.

The consumption of mussels in Galicia dates back to at least the eighth century BC. The Romans extended distribution to inland areas, but for many centuries mussels were very much food for the poor. In the eighteenth century, however, they began appearing on aristocratic tables, when the Mayor of Santiago declared, 'Its meat is second only to the oyster.' Experiments in farming started a century later, based around the old oyster beds. The first modern cultivation from rafts was in 1945, when the Marquis of Aranda floated the first raft, or *barea*, in the Arousa estuary. The results were impressive, and today the area around the Rías Baixas produces more than ninety-five per cent of Spanish mussels, making it the largest producer in Europe. Galician mussels were the first seafood to be protected under European legislation, and the industry is tightly regulated. The industry is tightly controlled, and Galician mussels were the first seafood in Europe to be protected under European legislation. The *bareas* are privately owned and although each one can be sold, no new ones can be established.

From the air, the tethered rafts, from which the mussels are cultivated on dangling ropes, look like giant stepping-stones across the open water; from the shore, they resemble an armada of surfaced submarines. On the boat owned by José Manuel Naveiro Pérez, a founder member of Amegrove, the first mussel producers' cooperative in Galicia, we watched his son Francisco skip nimbly across the grid of slippery eucalyptus logs. Working rapidly, he attached a weighty cluster of mussels to the winch that would raise them out of the water like inky sea serpents.

The mussels are harvested throughout the year, and taken directly from the rafts to the purification, grading and packing plants where they are kept on seawater ice. The *rías*, enclosed by strands of golden sand and slopes of dark green trees, have proved the perfect breeding grounds because the sheltered beds are lower than the sea, supplying a natural supply of plankton, minerals and oxygen on which the hungry little bivalves can fatten for eighteen months. The result is a purple-black triangular shell, as sharply pointed as a prehistoric axe-head, enclosing a juicy nugget of apricot flesh that turns a vivid, smoked-salmon colour when cooked. Yet despite the outstanding quality, the industry has its problems. Cheap competition from Chile and China has undercut the market, especially in the important canning and processed food sector. And, although the pure Galician waters have recovered from the *Prestige* disaster, resentment over poor compensation and slow government action is still keenly felt.

At the *fiesta*, the Virgin finished her journey with a paddle – carried with steely determination by the young people of O Grove, wading up to their ankles in the slipway. She looked out to sea, before turning to face the crowds on the jetty who serenaded her in song and dance. The procession regrouped to see her safely home. The funfair had just opened for the night, at an open-air concert young and old were dancing in the fading light. The town's restaurants were doing a brisk trade in mussels, oysters, razor clams, boiled octopus sprinkled with *pimentón* and saffron rice with lobster that would continue until the early hours. It had been a good day. Thanks, of course, to the Virgin of the Carmen.

ABOVE: GRAN HOTEL, A TOXA. RIGHT: *LA FIESTA DEL CARMEN*, O GROVE

Steamed Mussels

SERVES 4

Dolores 'Loli' Barreiro, of the Restaurant Finisterre in O Grove, is a lively, energetic lady with a big smile who presides over the tiny kitchen of the family restaurant, long renowned for its seafood. *'Llevo la batuta* – I'm the boss here,' she teases the staff.

'I only use mussels from my family's own raft, so I know exactly where they come from. These are really dark and shiny, so it shows just how fresh they are. First, you use a knife or scissors to trim the mussels of their beards or you can pull them off with your hands, then give them a good scrub and rinse. Don't use any that are broken or open. *¡Mira!* you can tell the age of the mussel from the rings on the shell. If it's a good, mature one, then it will feel nice and heavy in your hand.

'Place the mussels (about 1 kg/2 lb 4 oz) in a wide flat pan – it's best if they're in one layer so they cook evenly, then add a long spiral of lemon rind, 2 fresh bay leaves and a ladle of water so they don't burn. Place the pan over a high heat. The aim is to open the mussels quickly – if the heat is low they will only open slowly and the juices will evaporate. As soon as they open they are ready, but don't use any that haven't opened. You don't need any salt with these mussels, they already taste of the sea.'

Mussels *Vinagreta*

Loli points out that this popular first course needs to be quite sharp and vinegary, so it 'opens the appetite'.

SERVES 4

1 kg/2 lb 4 oz freshly cooked mussels on the half shell (see left)

FOR THE *VINAGRETA*:
6–7 tablespoons olive oil
3 tablespoons white wine vinegar

1 small mild onion, very finely chopped
½ green pepper, very finely diced
½ red pepper, very finely diced
1 hard-boiled egg, very finely chopped
1 tablespoon fresh parsley, very finely chopped
Sea salt

Whisk the olive oil with a good pinch of sea salt, then add the vinegar followed by the remaining *vinagreta* ingredients. Mix well and taste. Add more eggs or vinegar, as wished.

Arrange the mussels on a serving dish and spoon over the *vinagreta*. Serve at room temperature.

ABOVE: (LEFT TO RIGHT) JOSÉ MANUEL NAVEIRO PÉREZ ON HIS *BATEA*; SORTING MUSSELS AT THE AMGROVE PURIFICATION PLANT. RIGHT: MUSSELS *VINAGRETA*

Creamy Mussel and Prawn Soup

The lush, green – and frequently rainy – interior of magical Galicia is wonderful dairy country, notable for milk, butter and cheese. This rich, slightly retro recipe combines the best of land and sea.

SERVES 4

1 kg/2 lb 4 oz mussels	15 ml/½ fl oz *Brandy de Jerez*
500 g/1 lb 2 oz cooked prawns	1 litre/1¾ fl oz fish stock
1 large onion, finely chopped	2 bay leaves
75 g/2¾ oz butter	150 ml/5½ fl oz single cream
4 tablespoons tomato sauce	Salt
or *pasata*	Chopped fresh parsley

Scrub and rinse the mussels well, removing the beards. Discard any broken or open ones. Steam the mussels according to the recipe on page 96, then drain, reserving the natural juices. When cool enough to handle, remove most the mussels from the shell (discarding any that have not opened), keeping a handful in their shells to use as garnish.

Melt the butter in a large saucepan and gently fry the onion until soft, without browning. Stir in the tomato sauce, and add the brandy. Once the alcohol has evaporated, add the stock and the reserved mussel liquid. Add the bay leaves and salt. Simmer for 20 minutes.

Keeping the heat low, add the cream, mussels and prawns. Allow the seafood to heat through, but do not boil. Serve sprinkled with parsley and garnished with the reserved mussels.

Mussel and Saffron *Empanada*

The *empanada* dates back to the time of the Goths, and in Galicia it is not so much a pie or pasty as a full-blown cult. There are books and websites devoted to the subject, and a dazzling choice of dough, fillings, shapes and techniques. In this recipe, the pinch of *pimentón* in the dough adds a subtle flavour and gives the pastry a rich, burnished tint.

MAKES A 23 CM/9 INCH PIE

FOR THE DOUGH:

500 g/1 lb 2 oz flour

1 teaspoon salt

1 teaspoon *pimentón de la Vera*

1 heaped teaspoon fast-action
    dried yeast

100 ml/3½ fl oz oil (olive or
    sunflower, as preferred)

200 ml/7 fl oz warm water

Mix the dry ingredients, and slowly add the oil and water. Combine well, until the dough is smooth and forms a ball that comes away from the sides of the mixing bowl. Cover and set aside for an hour while you make the filling.

FOR THE FILLING:

500 g/1 lb 2 oz onions, chopped

2 tablespoons olive oil

1 large pinch of saffron
    filaments, lightly crushed and
    soaked in a little hot water

1 kg/2 lb 4 oz mussels

Salt

1 beaten egg

Preheat the oven to 180°C/350°F/Gas Mark 4.

Heat the oil in a frying pan and cook the onions very slowly for 30–40 minutes, until beautifully caramelized.

When the onions are nearly ready, stir in the saffron and a little salt. Remove from the pan with a slotted spoon and set aside.

While the onions are cooking, steam the mussels according to the recipe on page 96, preferably substituting Albariño wine for the water. Discard any mussels that have not opened and remove the rest from their shells. Set aside.

Divide the dough in half. On a floured work surface, roll out one half thinly (about ½ cm/4 inch thick) and use to line a greased 23 cm/ 9 inch pie tin. The pastry circle should be large enough to overlap the edges, but cut off excessive overhang.

Put the onions into the pie tin and top with the mussels.

Roll out the other half of the dough and cover the pie. Press the pastry together and roll the edges inwards with a crimping motion, to seal the pie. If wished, decorate with a lattice made from leftover strips of pastry.

Brush the pie with beaten egg. Prick the top with a fork and bake for 40 minutes. Leave to settle for 10 minutes before turning out of the pan. Serve warm or at room temperature.

Baked Mussels in Tomato and Olive Sauce

SERVES 4 AS A STARTER, 2 AS A MAIN COURSE

1 kg/2 lb 4 oz mussels

300 ml/10 fl oz Albariño wine

6 shallots, finely chopped

2 garlic cloves, finely chopped

2 tablespoons olive oil

100 g/3½ oz black olives, stoned
    and chopped

100 ml/3½ fl oz tomato sauce
    or *pasata*

15 g/½ oz fresh parsley, chopped

2 tablespoons dried
    breadcrumbs

Salt and black pepper

Preheat the oven to 200°C/400°F/Gas Mark 6.

Scrub and rinse the mussels well, removing the beards. Discard any that are open or broken. Steam according to the recipe on page 96, substituting wine for the water. Alternatively, bring the wine to the boil, add the mussels, cover and cook for a few minutes, shaking the pan occasionally.

Once cooked, discard any unopened mussels. Remove one half of each shell and arrange the mussels on the remaining half shells in four individual earthenware or heatproof dishes. Strain the cooking liquid and reserve.

Fry the shallots and garlic in the oil without letting them colour. Add the reserved liquid and bring to the boil. Cook over a medium-high heat until reduced by half. Add the olives, tomato sauce, parsley, salt and pepper. Simmer for 2–3 minutes, and pour over the mussels.

Sprinkle with the breadcrumbs and bake in the preheated oven for 10 minutes. Serve hot, with plenty of bread to mop up the juices.

LA RIOJA: pears

an *exaltación* of pears

'We're only a little town, and we haven't got much money,' said the old lady next to me, 'but we've got a big heart!' and promptly kissed me on both cheeks. Even the town's most ardent supporters cannot pretend that Rincón de Soto is the most picturesque in La Rioja but, as the mayor's wife added, 'What we lack in beauty, we make up for in people.'

It was true. Rincón may be little more than a main *plaza*, a modern town hall, a church and a railway line, but it has a kind and generous community and a proud, go-ahead local authority. The economy is based on kitchen units and agriculture, and if Rincón is now on the map, it is due to their determined success in gaining D.O. status for the pears that have been grown on the banks of the Ebro, one of Spain's

greatest rivers, for centuries. As Sixto Cabezón of the Rincón Pear Association explained, 'In spring, the orchards are beautiful, decked out like a bride in white, but too many have been simply abandoned. European recognition help us position the fruit in a competitive market, but it also encourages young people to remain on the land and shows them there is a future in farming. This gives us a product we can take pride in. After all, we must have faith in ourselves.'

Rincón de Soto lies at the eastern end of Spain's smallest mainland region, near Calahorra, once an important Roman town famed for its circus and chariot races, and later for its cathedral. Here, in the Rioja Baja, a gently terraced swathe of fertile fields, orchards and plane trees with ever-dancing leaves, the famous vines take second place to pears, peaches, cherries, cauliflowers, onions, sprouts and

OPPOSITE: RIOJAN PEAR ORCHARD: RINCÓN DE SOTO AND FRUIT ORCHARDS. ABOVE: CONFERENCE PEARS

cardoons. The growing area is defined by a natural margin: the river that separates it from the mountains of Navarre to the north, and the craggy, Riojan hills further south where a network of dinosaur footprints remains eerily well preserved.

The annual *Festival de la Pera* takes place at the end of September, when they also celebrate the feast-day of San Miguel, the town's patron saint. The main street is closed off for the *encierro*, a hugely popular bull-running event of the sort held throughout northern Spain; cheering, grey-haired grannies, critical connoisseurs, mad, macho runners of all ages, and hot chorizo sausage on bread for everyone. Equally anticipated, if slightly less frenzied, is the pear cookery competition. The standard is high, and the awards ceremony has all the tension and jumps-for-joy of any close-fought contest. Afterwards, the town feasts on pears poached in red Rioja wine and parties until the small hours. A day, indeed, of *exaltación*.

In the small family orchards there are still fruiting trees that were planted in 1936, at the start of the Civil War. The remains of a sixteenth-century dam, the first in Spain to bring irrigation to the *huerta*, spans the Ebro. There had been an unusually high amount of spring rain the year of my visit, as well as autumnal hailstorms, but the farmers had managed to save most of the crop. The good news was that the fruit was of exceptional quality and size. In Spain, the general preference is for large Conference pears, although many still favour the delicate flavour of the smaller Blanquilla.

In 1747 the latter was enjoyed at the court of Philip V, where it was described as 'an exquisite fruit', and the royal pastry-cook recommended it for drying, confits or preserving in syrup. Sometimes known as a 'water pear', the Blanquilla is crisp, juicy and aromatic; as it ripens it becomes highly perfumed and meltingly soft, and the bright, lime-green skin takes on a reddish tinge. The Blanquilla, however, is more difficult to grow, and nearly disappeared in the 1960s as agriculture became more intensive, largely replaced by green-yellow, naturally russeted Conference pears with sweet, buttery flesh. For both these highly prized Rincón pears, though, it is the specific local geographic and climatic conditions that give them their special balance of sweetness and acidity, their keeping qualities and a texture that holds its shape well when cooked. Francis Paniego, a brilliant young Riojan chef, for example, cooks Conferences with meat and Blanquillas with fish at Echaurren, his acclaimed, innovative restaurant in the mountain village of Ezcaray.

During the harvest, the farmers work from dawn till dusk. The pears are delicate and easily bruised, and each fruit must be individually and precisely picked, held by the base and raised upwards so the stalk snaps clean from the branch and remains intact. They are transported within six hours, in padded containers, to one of the local packing stations where teams of women clean, grade and arrange them in perfect formation, each one a swaddled, green *infanta*. Remedios Jiménez, the bossy, eagle-eyed supervisor of the one I visited on the outskirts of Rincón, fired dangerous volleys of questions at me: 'So, Clarissa, what is your favourite food in Spain? ... So, Clarissa, how do you like our pears?...' I was happy to bite into a just-picked pear by way of answer.

Pears are not always an easy fruit to judge, we agreed, but as Remedios fiercely emphasized, 'If more people ate fruit when they were properly ripe, then there would be a lot more eaten! People just don't know what they're missing.'

ABOVE: PEAR PACKING STATION, RINCÓN DE SOTO. RIGHT: (CLOCKWISE FOM TOP LEFT) WATCHING THE BULL-RUNNING; AWAITING THE RESULTS OF THE PEAR COOKERY COMPETITION, FESTIVAL DE LA PERA; ENTRY IN THE PEAR COOKERY COMPETITION; FESTIVAL PEARS IN RIOJA WINE

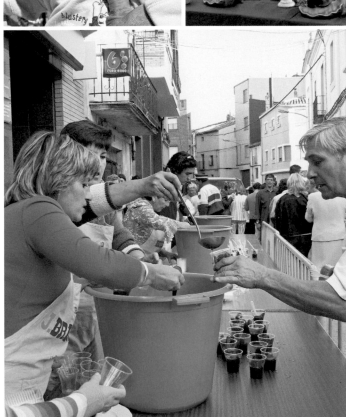

Olla Gitana

Olla means a tall, pot-bellied cooking pot, and this vibrant autumnal stew probably originates with the Romany travellers who arrived in Spain in the 1450s, settling mostly in Andalusia. A stew for days when there was little meat for the pot, this is vegetarian more by default than by choice. Today the vegetarian ethos is slowly spreading beyond cities such as Barcelona, although in many a *pueblo* ham is still classed as a vegetable, and they would probably regard this as a good dish to serve before a juicy lamb chop or veal escalope.

SERVES 4

150 g/5½ oz chickpeas

150 g/5½ oz white beans

250 g/9 oz green beans, sliced

1 butternut squash or a small pumpkin, peeled, seeded and cubed

1 medium carrot, sliced

2 Conference pears, peeled, cored and chopped

2 bay leaves

1 litre/1¾ pints vegetable stock

100 ml/3½ fl oz olive oil

1 large onion, diced

2 garlic cloves, diced

1 small slice of stale country or sourdough bread, with the crust cut off and fried in 1 tablespoon oil

25 g/1 oz toasted almonds

A pinch of saffron, lightly crushed and soaked in a little hot water

3 medium tomatoes, peeled and chopped

½–1 tablespoon *pimentón de la Vera*

2–3 sprigs fresh mint, chopped

Salt and black pepper

Soak the chickpeas and beans overnight. Next day, drain them, put them in a pot with fresh water and bring to the boil. Simmer for about 30 minutes, until soft, then drain and place in a large casserole (or an *olla*, if you have one).

Add the green beans, squash or pumpkin, carrot, pears, bay leaves and stock. Season with salt and pepper. Bring to the boil and simmer for 15–20 minutes, until everything is tender.

Heat the oil in a frying pan and cook the onion slowly for at least 15 minutes, until soft and golden. Meanwhile, pound the garlic, bread, almonds, saffron and a pinch of salt in a mortar until well combined. Stir in a ladle of stock from the bean pot.

Add the tomatoes to the onions and fry over a medium heat for another 5 minutes. Stir in the *pimentón* and cook for 1 minute. Add the onions and tomatoes to the bean pot, cook for about 5 minutes, then stir in the contents of the mortar. Simmer a little longer, and check the seasoning. Serve sprinkled with chopped mint.

Duck Breast with Honey-Spiced Pears

Based on an entry in the Rincón pear cookery competition, the success of this dish depends on the delicate balance of sweet and savoury flavours.

SERVES 2

2 duck breasts

Olive oil

1 tablespoon butter

2 tablespoons honey

3 cloves

1 tablespoon mixed peppercorns (white, green and pink)

2 ripe Conference pears, peeled, cored and quartered

Juice of 1 lemon

Salt

Fry the duck breast in a little olive oil (15–20 minutes, depending on thickness and preference). Set aside to rest for 5 minutes, then slice the duck and arrange on warm serving plates.

Melt the butter in a small saucepan over medium heat and add the honey and spices. Cook gently for a few minutes, until the honey melts and starts to bubble. Add the pears and turn gently in the buttery mixture until the edges start to caramelize. Add the lemon juice and a little salt.

Remove the pears from the pan and arrange alongside the duck. Strain the sauce and drizzle it over the duck.

Pear and *Jamón Serrano* Wraps

Another idea from the cookery competition. Mix some cream or curd cheese with a little, mashed blue cheese, chopped walnuts and peeled, diced pears. Spread on slices of *jamón serrano*, and roll up in tubes. Tie decoratively, if wished, with chives.

RIGHT: DUCK BREAST WITH HONEY-SPICED PEARS

Pears Poached in *Moscatel* and Spices

This is based on a recipe from María Pilar Hernández Fernández of Rincón de Soto.

SERVES 4

4 whole large (or 8 small) firm
   Conference or Blanquilla
   pears, peeled
750 ml/1½ pints *moscatel* wine
A few black peppercorns

3 cloves
Juice of 1 lemon
1 cinnamon stick
Toasted, chopped almonds

Place the pears in a saucepan that is just large enough to allow them to remain upright.

Pour the wine over the pears and add all the other ingredients, except the almonds. Bring to boiling point, cover the pan, and simmer for 30 minutes or until tender.

Serve sprinkled with almonds, and also, if wished, some strained syrup.

ABOVE: (LEFT TO RIGHT) CALHORRA TOWN CENTRE; FESTIVAL POSTER, RINCÓN DE SOTO. LEFT: PEARS POACHED IN *MOSCATEL* AND SPICES

Rioja Pear Cake

SERVES 4

200 g/7 oz softened butter
200 g/7 oz golden caster sugar,
   plus 1 tablespoon
4 medium eggs, separated
1 generous teaspoon vanilla
   extract
200 g/7 oz self-raising flour

8 Conference or Blanquilla
   pears, peeled, sliced and
   lightly poached in red Rioja
   wine with sugar and
   cinnamon to taste
2 tablespoons chopped walnuts
Salt
Whipped cream, to serve

Preheat the oven to 180°C/350°F/Gas Mark 4.

Cream the butter and sugar together, then beat in the egg yolks one by one, followed by the vanilla extract. Add the flour and stir until well combined.

Whisk the egg whites with a pinch of salt until snowy. Carefully fold them into the cake mixture. Pour into a round, buttered 23 cm/9 inch-deep cake tin with a removable base.

Drain the pears (saving the liquid) and arrange them in a neat pattern over the top of the cake. Sprinkle with the walnuts and a tablespoon of sugar. Bake for 40–50 minutes, until the top is well risen (although it will shrink back down when you remove it from the oven), and a skewer comes out clean.

Heat the syrupy red wine until it reduces, and serve with the cake along with some whipped cream.

MALLORCA:
black pigs and *sobrassada*

black pigs

Although George Sand wrote with excessive spite about her turbulent winter in Mallorca in 1838, she did (partially) hit the mark with her comments about the island's love of the pig, which they cooked in every imaginable form and manner. The local diet, she noted, was based on thousands of different dishes, including hundreds of black pudding, all made from pork, including a seemingly blameless fruit tart. Everything, however, she shrieked, was spiced with such excessive ferocity that each innocent mouthful became a potential death-trap. She exaggerated hysterically, of course, as with every other aspect of her blighted sojourn there in the company of Frédéric Chopin and her two children, but the comment is nevertheless rooted in a reality that still exists today.

Mallorca has stoically endured waves of invaders and occupiers, remaining a backwater until well into the twentieth century when mass tourism transformed the local economy, afflicted parts of the coast with mega-resorts and resulted in the M word becoming a synonym for lager louts and breakfast just like mother makes. Yet the traditional cooking of the island is individual, intriguing and little known. As Elizabeth Carter notes in her *Majorcan Food and Cooking*, it derives from a peasant tradition, and although similar to Catalan cuisine in its repertoire of rich, compound dishes, is generally more down to earth.

It is to the island's credit, however, that it has not only halted the excesses of destructive, bargain-basement tourism, but has re-invented its image, helped by the Spanish royal family, the writings of the Graves family and several film-star holiday-home owners. Outside Palma, an animated city of shops,

OPPOSITE: BLACK PIG; *SOBRASSADA* HANGING FROM BAMBOO POLES,

ABOVE: JOAN MARTORELL, NEAR FELANITX

restaurants and old mansions dominated by the Gothic cathedral, Mallorca remains a gentle island with a pastoral landscape of orange trees and blue bays, pretty Moorish towns and silvery mountains.

They say you can always spot a true islander at the airport departures hall: they will be the ones carrying octagonal boxes of *ensaimada* (airy coils of sweet yeast and lard pastry), bags of Inca biscuits made with olive oil, and armfuls of *sobrassada*, their beloved sausage. The word sausage is not quite right — *sobrassada* is half sausage, half paste; sticky, sweet and spicy at the same time; smooth and soft enough to spread on toasted bread. Traditionally it is made from the native black pig, a breed that has been saved from near-extinction in a remarkable conservation success story.

This technique of seasoning ground pork is said to date back to Roman times, and the word is said to originate either from the Italian *soppressa*, meaning pressed, or, as Tomás Graves suggests in *Bread & Oil*, from the Latin *sale presata*, preserved in salt. However, under the centuries of Muslim rule in Spain, pig-rearing took a back seat, and it was not until 1403 that the term *sobrassada* was first recorded. Towards the

end of the eighteenth century, the introduction of *pimentón* from the Americas gave the sausage its distinctive orange-red colour, spicy flavour and leg-up into the great pantheon of Spanish *embutidos*. Essentially the process, and the simple partnership of island, pig and sausage, has changed little since then.

At the turn of the twentieth century there were around 70,000 black pigs in Mallorca. Fattened on figs, carob and barley as well as prickly pears and boiled sweet potatoes, the pigs were butchered in the winter and most of the meat was turned into *sobrassada*, enough to feed a family over the whole year. Its reputation spread, manufacturers sprang up, and *sobrassada* was shipped to Barcelona and Valencia, and as far as Cuba and Puerto Rico. Yet, only fifty years later, both product and pig were on the point of disappearing. A victim of its own success, the sausage had been copied by industrial producers on the mainland who flooded the market with a cheap, inferior version made from intensively farmed white pigs that are more fertile and quicker to fatten. On the 'if you can't beat them, join them' principle, the local manufacturers responded by importing their own white pigs and producing an equally bad sausage.

As tourism changed the nature of the island's economy, *sobrassada*, along with other Balearic products such as capers, samphire, almonds, sweet white onions, purple carrots, light green peppers, luscious dried apricots and figs, small, firm pears *de Sant Joan* and many varieties of tomatoes (including the tiny hanging tomatoes that miraculously stay fresh throughout the winter), was commercially sidelined in the headlong rush to build beach hotels serving the 'international' menus demanded by the new sun 'n' sand *conquistadores*. No one seemed interested in the poor little black pig when there were so many two-legged cash cows to milk.

Happily, at the beginning of the 1980s, a heroic rescue plan was mounted by Sebastien Simo Planes, a young businessman who decided to open a shop in Palma selling the very best *sobrassada*. But to get the very best, you need a black pig. So Planes persuaded four farmers to breed from the few specimens left,

ABOVE : MANUFACTURER'S STREET SIGN, FELANITX

OPPOSITE: SCENES FROM A RURAL PIG-KILLING IN THE INTERIOR OF MALLORCA

shouldering the financial risk and paying in advance. At the same time, several restaurants introduced old local dishes on to their menus. The time was right, but it took several years for the tide to turn, and for the producers to secure European protection for the *Sobrassada de Mallorca Cerdo Negro*, as well as the *Sobrassada de Mallorca*, made from extensively reared white pigs.

One mild spring day I found myself staring into the equally startled, comic little face of a frisky young porker who was undecided as to whether my boots were an unexpected windfall or something his mother should have warned him about. Friendly and inquisitive, his flat, floppy ears shaded his face like a double-brimmed baseball cap. Delicate trotters supported a rotund frame, the pink skin visible through bar-code strands of dark hair. Two strange protuberances dangled under the pronounced snout, like loose sideburns. He was quickly joined by a dozen other, equally sociable, siblings. Squeal, snort, snuffle. Then, turning corkscrew tail, they were off in a piggy pack to explore pastures new and to find more exciting things to eat.

We were near Felanitx in the east of the island, famous for wine, ceramics and pearls. The farm was old, built of honey-coloured stone, with a single, high Moorish palm tree like a flagpole. There are now around thirty farmers rearing 2,500 black pigs on the island, and Joan Martorell had switched three years previously from cows to pigs in response to the growing market. He looked around, across neat fields sectioned with dry-stone walls, towards a line of low hills; the earth was vivid with lime-green grass, and the almond trees were in fragile blossom. '¡Mira! How tranquil and beautiful it is here. Breathe deep, it's good for your health! Twenty years ago, I would never have believed I'd end up with pigs, of all things. No, I don't miss the cows, I'm happy with my pigs. They look after themselves, but then, if you treat any animal well, they won't let you down.'

I had come with vet Ramón García, who was there to clip an identifying tag to a new litter that would trace them from field to plate. He explained that the pigs were intensively reared for nine months, then their diet would be enhanced with figs, pulses and barley for a further three months to ensure the sweet flesh and creamy fat that gives *sobrassada* its special quality. I asked whether the meat was ever eaten fresh. 'Well, some people have started to cook suckling pigs but, really, the meat is too fatty. The black pig is best suited to preserving, particularly in the form of *sobrassada*.'

Many families still make their own *sobrassada*, and the technique in both home and factory remains much the same. A mix of lean and fatter meat from the loin, fillet and leg is coarsely minced, flavoured with *pimentón*, sweet or spicy, and sea salt, and stuffed into natural casing. The sausages are swiftly and expertly tied with string by dexterous women workers, and strung from bamboo poles laid across wooden racks to cure for a minimum of forty days.

Once the *pimentón* would have been made from the island's own mild red peppers, but there are no commercial growers left and, according to Sebasti Escales of Embutits Escales, the spice is now imported from Murcia. The sea salt, however, still comes from the flats that have been in production since Phoenician times, but the key, he added, is the air of the island, salty, soft and slightly damp. Producers differ in the artisan details but, like business anywhere, sometimes you feel you just never can win. As Antoni Gomis Ferrer, the lively young commercial director of Caín Balaguer, a producer in the ancient hill town of Artá, half-jokingly sighed, 'In Palma they'll say a *sobrassada* is too *picante*, and in one of the mountain villages they'll say the same sausage is far too bland!' There are seven shapes of *sobrassada*, ranging from freshly cured slender loops served fried at the January fiestas held after the winter pig-killing, to Punch and Judy truncheons, bulging packets, rugby balls, balloons and vast cushions packed into large intestines, bladders and stomachs. Once cured, the sausages will keep for up to a year.

ABOVE: ADDING WATER TO THE COOK POT FROM THE FARM WELL, MALLORCA

RIGHT: MAKING HOME-MADE *SOBRASSADA* AFTER THE PIG-KILLING

Sobrassada is an indispensable part of the Mallorcan kitchen, added to soups and stews, lending flavour to rice, seafood and vegetable dishes; it can even be sweetened with honey and wine or used as an intriguing Arabic-style filling for *ensaimadas*. Antoni, however, said his favourite recipe was to toss some artichokes, mushrooms and tomatoes in olive oil, bake for ten minutes, crack over some eggs, sprinkle with pieces of sausage and bake again until the eggs were set and 'everything is perfect!' Sebasti, on the other hand, eats his *sobrassada* spread simply on unsalted country bread, 'If you've got a good product, you don't need to mess about with it.'

POSTSCRIPT

A number of talented chefs on Mallorca are finding imaginative ways of using this age-old product in their cooking. A few years ago, Tomeu Caldentey returned to his home town of Sant Llorenç and opened a suave, contemporary restaurant in a converted mill. Es Moli Den Bou quickly gained a Michelin star for cooking which is refined but essentially simple, clear and true, based on Mallorcan ingredients. I sampled a meal there in which every course contained *sobrassada*, from a glorious combination of salt cod, artichokes and baby octopus, to quails with *sobrassada* and honey. As Tomeu said, 'I want to go beyond the bread and spread image of *sobrassada*. It gives a deep, savoury note to Mallorcan cuisine, and although it is never the basis of a dish, it is important for special flavour. Our grandmothers would always add a little bit to any dish they were cooking. The result is always individual; it reflects our personality.'

This simple assembly is based on one of the dishes: spread a little *sobrassada* on each plate and top with a slice of warm, toasted goat's cheese. Add a little chunky apple purée and some finely chopped black olives or *pansides* (wrinkled Mallorcan olives flavoured with oil, lemon juice, garlic, bay leaf and sweet paprika). Drizzle with olive oil.

Pork Chops with Broad Bean, Tomato and Mint Sauce

Broad beans are grown all over the Balearics and Catalonia, often planted between the almond and olive trees. The sweetness of broad beans, especially young ones, goes particularly well with pork, but the recipe can also be made with lamb chops.

SERVES 4

4 large pork chops

1 kg/2 lb 4 oz broad beans in the pod (to give about 225 g/8 oz shelled weight)

2 tablespoons olive oil

1 medium onion, finely chopped

1 large garlic clove, finely chopped

100 g/3½ oz *sobrassada*, cut into small pieces (optional, or use soft chorizo)

50 g/1¾ oz *panceta*, cubed (or *jamón serrano*, in strips)

30 ml/1 fl oz white wine

300 g/10½ oz tomato sauce (or *passata*)

25 g/1 oz fresh mint, chopped

Salt

Boil the broad beans until tender, then drain and leave until cool enough to pop the bright green inner bean out of the tough, outer skin (unless the beans are young and just picked).

Heat the oil in a frying pan and cook the onion gently for at least 10 minutes, until soft and starting to turn golden. Add the garlic, followed by the *sobrassada* and *panceta*, and cook for another 5 minutes. Add the white wine and cook for a few minutes more to allow the alcohol to evaporate. Add the tomato sauce, broad beans and a little salt, and leave to simmer while you grill or fry the chops.

Add the mint to the sauce and serve with the chops.

Pork and Spinach Meatballs

This recipe uses pork, but *albóndigas*, Spanish meatballs, can also be made with pork mixed with veal, beef or lamb, according to the preference of each *ama de casa* (housewife). These are good with a spicy tomato sauce.

MAKES ABOUT 24 SMALL MEATBALLS

400 g/14 oz minced pork (twice-minced is best)

50 g/1¾ oz *sobrassada*, cut into small pieces (optional, or use finely chopped soft chorizo)

400 g/14 oz fresh spinach, cooked, drained and finely chopped

1 large egg, lightly beaten

1–2 tablespoons fine breadcrumbs

Flour, for coating

Olive oil, for frying

Salt, black pepper and grated nutmeg

Mix the pork, *sobrassada*, spinach, egg and breadcrumbs and season well – altogether a job best done by hand.

Shape the mixture into balls about the size of a large walnut. Dust with flour and fry in hot olive oil until brown and crusty on both sides.

ABOVE: OUTSIDE THE CATHEDRAL, PALMA, MALLORCA

LEFT: PORK CHOPS WITH BROAD BEAN, TOMATO AND MINT SAUCE

Coca de Trempo

The Mallorcan answer to pizza, except that *coca* is not usually eaten hot and never contains cheese. *Coca* is a savoury pastry of ancient origin and is traditionally cooked in an outdoor, wood-fired oven. The dough, typically enriched with lard, is based on one in Elizabeth Carter's *Majorcan Food and Cookery*. Today, lard is regarded as a bit old-fashioned, and many recipes use just oil and yeast, or shortcrust pastry. Toppings vary according to the cook's imagination. *Trempo*, which refers to summer vegetables, is perhaps the most common, but other permutations include onions, garlic, peppers and tomatoes; Swiss chard, tomatoes, and onions; spinach, pine nuts and raisins; pork loin and peppers. Sweet *cocas* are made for Saint John's Day in June with candied fruit and nuts. You will need a circular, lightly oiled 34 cm/14 inch baking tray.

SERVES 6–8

FOR THE DOUGH:

500 g/1 lb 2 oz strong bread flour
1 teaspoon easy-bake yeast (or equivalent)
50 g/1¾ oz lard, cut into small pieces
2 tablespoons olive oil
150 ml/5 fl oz warm water
Salt

FOR THE TOPPING:

1 red pepper, finely sliced
1 green pepper, finely sliced
1 courgette, finely sliced
1 onion, finely sliced
75 g/2¾ oz *sobrassada*, cut into pieces (optional, or use soft chorizo)
Olive oil
Salt

Mix the flour and yeast either by hand or in an electric mixer with a dough hook, then add the lard, oil, water and a good pinch of salt (this order may vary depending on the variety of yeast used – look at the packet instructions). Knead well until the dough forms a fairly smooth, elastic ball, then cover with a cloth and leave in a warm place for an hour or until the dough has doubled in size.

Mix the peppers, courgette and onion and dress with 1–2 tablespoons of oil and some salt. Set aside. Preheat the oven to 180°C/350°F/Gas Mark 4.

Once the dough has risen, knock it down and knead again. Place it on the baking tray and pat it out to fit. The dough should be fairly thin with a little raised edge. Prick the base with a fork.

Arrange the vegetables over the *coca*, dotting with pieces of *sobrassada*. Drizzle with olive oil. Bake for 40 minutes, until the dough is cooked and golden. Remove from the oven and sprinkle with a little more olive oil. Serve warm or at room temperature.

Pork and Cabbage Parcels

A richly-flavoured, favourite, Mallorcan family dish.

SERVES 4

8 slices of pork tenderloin (approx 125 g/4½ oz per person)
8 large green cabbage leaves with the stems removed (plus a few extras as stand-bys)
Olive oil
8 slices of *sobrassada* (or use soft *chorizo*)
8 slices of *butifarrón* (Mallorcan black pudding), or *morcilla* or other black pudding

1 large onion, finely chopped
125 g/4½ oz *panceta*, diced
3 garlic cloves, finely chopped
150 ml/5 fl oz white wine
400 g/14 oz ripe tomatoes, peeled, seeded and chopped
1 tablespoon raisins
1 tablespoon pinenuts
25 g/1 oz fresh parsley, finely chopped
Salt and black pepper

Blanch the cabbage leaves in boiling salted water for 1–2 minutes, then drain and lay them out to dry. Heat a little oil in a frying pan and gently fry the pork slices on both sides until just coloured.

Place a piece of pork on each leaf, and top each with a piece of *sobrassada* and black pudding. Wrap to form parcels, with the join underneath. If the pork is too large for the leaf, cut it in half and use the stand-by leaves to make extra parcels. Place side by side in a large, lightly oiled, heatproof dish.

Using the same pan in which the pork was cooked, gently fry the onion until soft, about 10 minutes, adding a little extra oil if necessary. Add the *panceta*, raise the heat to medium, and fry until golden. Add two-thirds of the garlic, cook until the aroma arises, then add the wine. Cook for 1–2 minutes, and add the tomatoes. Lower the heat and simmer until thick.

Stir in the raisins and pinenuts, and season lightly. Pour the sauce over the cabbage parcels until they are almost, but not completely, covered. Mix the remaining garlic with the parsley and scatter over the cabbage parcels. Cover the dish with either a lid or foil and simmer on top of the stove for an hour. (If preferred, cook in a low oven and remove the cover for the final 10 minutes).

RIGHT: COCA DE TREMPO

MURCIA: Calasparra rice

grains of rice

'First buy your rabbit,' instructed Señora María Martinez Novas, as she prepared to make *arroz con conejo*, a speciality of the small town of Calasparra in north-west Murcia. 'A live one, of course.'

On cue, as if from a conjuror's hat, Pedro, her soft-spoken husband, tenderly withdrew a furry four-legged creature from a well-tied plastic bag, holding it up by the hind legs for general inspection. We will draw a veil over the next few minutes, except to say that if ever I meet a scary monster rabbit in or out of my dreams, I now know where to aim the single karate chop, how to skin it with a Velcro-like rip, and gut it in one easy step. 'See, this way is kind, gentle and quick,' said Pedro. 'More natural than a factory. And the carcass is hardly damaged – which gives the rice a much better flavour!'

'Of course, you have to kill it the day before you're going to eat it,' added María, with the deftness of a celebrity TV chef suddenly producing a pot of chopped meat and stock she had prepared earlier. 'We use all the rabbit, the head, the neck, everything, it all adds to the taste. Sometimes we add snails, but today we're just going to make it with rabbit and peppers.'

Earlier, I had visited the Santuario de la Virgen de la Esperanza, after whom the town's largest rice cooperative is named. Murcia is one of the hottest regions of Spain, with the lowest rainfall, and the dramatic, wild countryside can be bleached and parched in summer, yet here, in a hidden mountain gulley two hours from the coast, beside the rocky river whose clear waters tumble on to work their magic on the

OPPOSITE: (LEFT TO RIGHT) WATER CHANNEL, RICE FIELDS, CALASPARRA; PAINTED WALL SIGN, RICE MILL, CALASPARRA, MURCIA CITY CENTRE. ABOVE: STITCHING RICE BAGS, LA ESPERANZA RICE MILL, CALASPARRA.

ancient rice-producing fields, there were shady pines, old olive trees, lush flowers and an air of serenity. On the plain far below there were orchards of peach and apricot trees; in early spring, they were bright with delicate blossom, shot through with drifts of purple wildflowers.

The shrine was hewn directly out of the cliff where the Virgin was said to have appeared in a vision to a local peasant, and the cave-like interior was filled with multicoloured banks of triangular floral arrangements. Every Sunday and holiday, especially at the September pilgrimage, the sanctuary is packed with families who have come to enjoy the rural scenery, splash in the crystal waters, picnic and eat *arroz con conejo* in the sanctuary's restaurant. Everyone in Murcia knows that in Calasparra you get not only the best rice in Spain, but also the cooks who know best how it should be prepared.

Calasparra is a small town with a big reputation. Of the two D.O. varieties of rice grown here, Balilla x Sollana (including brown and organic rice) and Bomba, the latter is the cream of the crop, highly prized but difficult to cultivate. The rice grows within a naturally limited stretch of land between the Sierra San

Miguel and the Segura and Mundo rivers, both popular for summer water-rafting. With great pride, the gentlemen of the Regulatory Council explained that the exceptional quality of the rice derives from the pure mountain water, altitude and traditional methods of cultivation. The lie of the land, a remarkable 500 metres above sea level, means the short, round grains are small and slow to ripen compared to other rice-producing areas. Yet each grain is a little round sponge that swells when cooked to three times its size; the result is rice of magnificent flavour, with individual grains that are both firm and yielding.

The town's microclimate brings hot, dry days and cold, humid nights, conditions that favour healthy plants. In addition, the 250 or so producers practise a system of crop rotation that is vitally important for the quality and regeneration of the soil. In a two-year cycle they alternate rice, wheat and legumes such as broccoli. The foliage from the latter is ploughed in after harvesting to provide natural fertilizer for the rice. 'This is very important,' stressed Antonio de Béjar Reverte, President of the Regulatory Council. 'We're very lucky that the quality of the soil in this area allows us to rotate the crops, which is one of the main reasons for the top quality of our rice.'

The Byzantines are thought to have introduced rice into Spain, but it was the Arabs who brought large-scale production to the Valencia region in the eighth century. In 1295, Fernando IV authorized the export of rice from Murcia to Mallorca and North Africa, but later monarchs prohibited the trade on the pretext that it would go to feed infidels. Over the centuries, production was also fraught with difficulties due to the vulnerability of the coastal plantations to malaria, but by the eighteenth century rice was established as an essential part of the regional culinary repertoire, and Spain is now the world's second largest growing area. In theory, it is possible to eat a different rice dish every day of the year. The ubiquitous paella is only the tip of a large mountain of rice-eating possibilities and techniques.

Throughout the rice-growing areas of the Levante, the basic network of Moorish irrigation and drainage is still in place. In Calasparra, river water that originates in mountain streams is diverted by means of a small dam into channels which open through old sluice gates into terraced plots that slope back down to the river. As a result, the water is constantly renewed and never stagnates. Calasparra

ABOVE: MURCIA TOWN HALL. OPPOSITE: (TOP LEFT TO RIGHT) MURCIA CATHEDRAL; STREET SCENE, MURCIA; FLOWER STALL, MURCIA CITY CENTRE; *TEATRO DE ROMEA*, MURCIA.

is lucky: elsewhere in the region, water is increasingly expensive and scarce as a result of the continued expansion of the great market gardens of Murcia's *huerta* and the proliferation of golf courses and tourist developments along the coast.

The rice year follows a reassuring rhythm. In April, the ground is prepared; each field, bordered by raised banks, forms part of the patchwork of brown squares that hug the winding riverbanks. By communal agreement, the fields are flooded later that month or in early May. After a tractor has ploughed the ground under the water, men roll up sleeves and trousers and wade through the fields, scattering the seeds by hand across the glassy squares of water that mirror the sun and sky like liquid chessboards.

As they grow, the shoots are thinned and replanted. In late June, the water is briefly drained and the ground weeded. Flooded once more, the spindly, gold-green plants are left to ripen slowly until the October harvest, when the water is drained yet again before the rice is picked. It is a method that has stood the test of time. As Señor Reverte said, 'Why should we change our methods? They've worked well for centuries. Why fix something that's not broken?'

Well, not quite. One thing that has changed since documents first recorded production methods in the fifteenth century is the method of harvesting. In the old days the fields were ploughed by oxen, the rice hand-picked and processed and transported by donkey, with virtually the whole town turning out to help. In the 1970s, simple machinery was introduced to do the job, but he is right that, in essence, the production of Calasparra rice has changed little over the years. And nobody misses the donkeys and mules. 'They might have been lovely to see, but believe me, they were most uncomfortable to ride!'

Once picked, the rice is taken to one of two mills in the town where it is dried naturally, so it can be stored without fermenting. It is then cleaned, husked, graded and polished, as necessary. A small production line of local women pack the rice into numbered cotton sacks, which they twist, hand-sew, tie and knot closed in a blur of nimble fingers. Locals buy their rice more prosaically – and more cheaply – in cellophane packs.

ABOVE: (LEFT TO RIGHT) MARÍA MARTINEZ NOVAS COOKING *ARROZ CON CONEJO*; CALASPARRA RICE BAGS.
OPPOSITE: BULLFIGHTING POSTERS, CALASPARRA

The Calasparra trademark was granted by royal decree in 1908 but, as its fame spread, others took unauthorized advantage of the name. In 1986 the rice became the first to gain European protection, but as Señor Reverte declared, 'The rice was top quality before and after we got the label. Nothing's changed, except no one else can pretend to sell it now.'

The general view was that elsewhere, mentioning no names but possibly beginning with V, labels were more important than quality. 'We're the other way round. We don't want to fight about it, but we're the *only* ones certified by the *national* department of agriculture. Our production will always be limited because of the amount of land we can use. We always run out of Bomba before the season ends, but we want it to be sold to people who appreciate it.'

The discussion had become animated, with the manager of the rice mill drawing helpful little diagrams to aid his explanations. They all burst out laughing when I remarked on the quality of the collection I was amassing. It put us in a good mood for lunch. As María cooked, they explained how the stock is absorbed by the starch in the *perla*, the heart of the rice. Cooking time is critical: the rice must be firm, yet the grains whole and soft. If overcooked, the *perla* breaks down and releases the starch, resulting in a mushy texture and spoilt flavour.

'The only thing Calasparra has in common with other short-grain rice is that it is white, but people must learn how to cook it properly,' emphasized Señor Reverte. 'If you prepare it according to other Spanish measures and timing, then it won't work. You have to use more water and cook it longer. It's very important. Be sure to stress that in your book.'

Calasparra Rice and Rabbit

This is based on the recipe María made with fresh rabbit; chicken makes a fair substitute, although the taste will differ. But at least you don't have to deal with the social niceties of finding a rabbit's head on your plate. Like many rice and *paella* dishes, it is best cooked over a wood fire, scented with rosemary and vine cuttings. Apart from the scent, this ensures that the bottom and sides of the pan are subject to constant heat. The dish, however, can be cooked perfectly well on an ordinary stove, using all the burners, or in two paella pans if you don't have a single huge one. Place each pan over two burners and turn around from time to time, in order to keep the heat even. Do the same if you scale down the ingredients and only use a single pan (this is easy as long as you keep the rice and liquid proportions the same).

Note, as a general rule, when using Calasparra Barilla x Sollana rice allow a ratio of 1 measure of rice to 3 or 3½ measures of liquid; if using Calasparra Bomba rice, allow a ratio of 1 measure of rice to 4 or 4½ measures of liquid. But making a good *arroz* or *paella* is a mathematical equation of volume, temperature, dimensions and quantities enough to baffle Archimedes. As my guide, José María García Soto of Murcia, told me, 'My mother has been preparing rice for forty years every Saturday. We NEVER order rice in a restaurant, because it's never as good as the rice we have at home. I have learnt how to do it from her; it takes time, but it's not difficult. You just have to learn how to do it properly.'

SERVES 10–12

Olive oil

1 rabbit, cut into small pieces and salted (or chicken, thighs for best flavour)

2 large ripe tomatoes, peeled, seeded and chopped

5 litres/9 pints water, lightly salted

1 kg/2 lb 4 oz Calasparra Bomba rice

2 large pinches of saffron filaments, lightly crushed and soaked in a little hot water

2 large red peppers, roasted, peeled and cut into broad strips

4 garlic cloves

A bunch of fresh parsley, chopped

Extra fresh parsley, to garnish (optional)

Heat some olive oil in a frying pan and brown the pieces of rabbit. Remove from the pan, then add the tomatoes to the pan and cook until soft. Set aside.

Put the water into a large pan and bring to the boil. Add the rabbit and cook for 20 minutes. Drain, reserving the stock. As María says, 'Not everyone takes the trouble to make the broth, so they use water for the rice instead, but of course it won't be so good.'

Reheat the tomatoes, and stir in the rice until it is lightly toasted and has absorbed all the surplus oil.

Put the stock and rabbit pieces into a *paella* pan (we're talking *muy grande* here – María used one about 1 metre/3 feet in diameter, propped on the special burners available in Spain for this purpose). Bring to the boil and sprinkle in the rice and tomatoes, saffron, garlic and parsley. Finally arrange the peppers over the top.

'Once the rice is in the pan, DON'T STIR. This is HERESY. ABSOLUTELY FORBIDDEN!! Just leave it alone. If you must, you can gently shake the pan by the two handles, but THAT'S IT.'

The rice must bubble fierce and fast on a high heat for 10 minutes (by the clock); imagine each little grain jumping for joy. Turn down the heat a little, and leave to cook for another 10 minutes.

When the time is up, turn off the heat, cover the pan with a clean cloth or foil and leave to rest for 15 minutes. This is VERY IMPORTANT, but 'the trick is to turn off the heat just before the rice is cooked, as it will keep on cooking in the pan. It's a question of judgement. You've got to learn the precise moment, that's where experience comes in. If it is cooked for too long, the rice will become like chewing gum. And NEVER add extra water. If all the liquid has evaporated before the 20 minutes are up, turn off the heat and cover the rice. It is ABSOLUTELY FORBIDDEN to add extra water.'

By now the rice should be ready to serve, but in fact it improves the longer it 'relaxes' in the pan. Which makes it perfect for seconds. Or thirds. Sprinkle with chopped parsley if you want it to look nice in a photo, but the refinement is unnecessary.

Murcian Vegetable and Salt Cod Paella

1 large ripe tomato, peeled, seeded and chopped
Olive oil
200 g/7 oz green beans, halved
200 g/7 oz cauliflower, separated into small florets
200 g/7 oz young broad beans, shelled
800 g/2 lb artichokes, trimmed and quartered (use preserved ones if fresh are unavailable)
4 shallots, chopped

200 g/7 oz salt cod, soaked, lightly pre-cooked and flaked
2 teaspoons *pimentón de la Vera*
A good pinch of saffron filaments, lightly crushed and soaked in a little hot water
400 g/14 oz Calasparra rice
1.5 litres/2¾ pints hot fish or vegetable stock
Salt

Salt cod needs to be soaked in cold water for 24–36 hours, with two or three changes of water, then drained and rinsed. Alternatively, use fresh white fish, in which case there is no need to pre-cook it.

SERVES 4

Soften the tomato in a little oil in a small pan, and set aside.

Heat enough oil to cover the bottom of a *paella* pan approximately 30 cm/12 inches wide. Add all the vegetables and fry over medium heat for about 10 minutes until they wilt. Add a little more oil if necessary. Stir in the tomato, salt cod, *pimentón*, saffron and salt. Add the rice, stirring it around until it is toasty, well-coloured and has absorbed any excess oil.

Pour in the hot stock, bring to the boil and cook for 20 minutes, reducing the heat half way through. Turn off the heat, cover with a clean cloth and leave to stand for 15 minutes before serving.

Rice with Monkfish, Chickpeas and Spinach

Another recipe from the flower-filled city of Murcia, dotted with Baroque churches and Moorish remains. During Holy Week, the astonishingly lifelike eighteenth-century sculptures of the Last Supper, normally on show in the Museo Salzillo, are carried in procession through the streets, with the table laid with fresh fruit and vegetables, roasted meat and fish, wine and bread, napkins and crystal glasses. For a classic Easter trinity, replace the monkfish in this recipe with salt cod.

SERVES 4–6

100 ml/3½ fl oz olive oil

1 large onion, finely chopped

1 large, ripe tomato, peeled, seeded and chopped

1 head of garlic, separated into unpeeled cloves

400 g/14 oz cooked chickpeas

80 g/3 oz spinach or Swiss chard

1 tablespoon *pimentón de la Vera*

200 ml/7 fl oz white wine

1 litre/1¾ pints hot fish stock

A large pinch of saffron filaments, lightly crushed and soaked in a little hot water

500 g/1 lb 2 oz monkfish, cut into large cubes and salted

400g/14 oz Calasparra rice

Salt

Lemon wedges, for serving

Heat the oil in a *paella* pan approximately 30cm/12 inches wide and gently soften the onion for at least 10 minutes without browning.

Add the tomato and cook for a minute or two before adding the garlic cloves and chickpeas. Add the spinach and stir until it wilts. Stir in the *pimentón* briefly, then add the wine, stock, saffron and salt. Bring up the boil and add the monkfish, followed by the rice. Cook over a medium heat for 10 minutes, then turn down the heat and simmer for another 10 minutes. Resist the temptation to stir.

Turn off the heat; cover the pan with a clean cloth, and leave to rest for 15 minutes. Serve with lemon wedges.

Cinnamon Rice Pudding

An all-time favourite Spanish dessert, this version of *arroz con leche* is based on one from Asturias, where they sprinkle the chilled rice with sugar and glaze it with a *quemador*, a heated metal plate attached to a long wooden handle. Follow with either a siesta or a *carajillo*, sharp black coffee laced with Spanish brandy.

SERVES 6

1 litre/1¾ pints full-fat milk (the creamier the better)

150 g/5½ oz Calasparra rice

200 ml/7 fl oz water

Pinch of salt

1 stick of cinnamon, snapped in half

A long strip of lemon peel (use a potato peeler)

100 g/3½ oz caster sugar

50g/1¾ oz unsalted butter

Ground cinnamon

Put the milk in a large saucepan and heat gently. Remove from the heat as soon as it reaches boiling point. In another, smaller pan heat the rice, water, salt, cinnamon and lemon peel over a medium-low heat until the rice has absorbed the water.

Add the rice, cinnamon and peel to the milk, and heat gently for about 40 minutes, stirring frequently, until the mixture is thick and creamy.

Stir in the sugar and butter. Remove the cinnamon sticks and lemon peel and serve cold, sprinkled with a little ground cinnamon.

NAVARRE: *piquillo* peppers

from the fields, to the tin

Real Madrid had lost the previous night to Bilbao, and spirits were slightly downcast at the Perón family factory in Lodosa, where the attached *cantina* doubled as a small shrine to their beloved team. *No importa*, there was plenty to do. It was one of the busiest times of the year, and they were working round the clock to roast, skin and can the town's most famous product: *pimientos del piquillo de Lodosa*. Lipstick-red, the peppers are hand-picked, sweet and fleshy. Roasted and preserved in their natural juice, the tiny, triangular shapes echo the shape and proud colour of the neck-scarves worn throughout Navarra at fiestas and bull-running. Throughout the town, the seductive, smoky scent of roasting peppers hung faintly in the air like the slipstream of a plane high in the clear, September sky.

The story is an unusual one. Too bitter to eat when raw, originally small amounts of *piquillos* were grown only for home consumption, to be either freshly roasted or conserved in containers, as first mentioned in the great cooking compendium, *El Practicón*, published in 1893. *Piquillo* means 'little beak', and the crop was negligible compared to the more widely grown *cuernos de cabra* (goat-horn peppers, so-called because of their shape). In the 1960s, however, Lodosa became a popular holiday spot for Basque families, and many took cans of *piquillo* peppers home with them as souvenirs. Their reputation grew, and more were planted, but the turning point came when a Lodosan chef, Julián Rivas, included them in the simple chops-and-peppers menu at his restaurant in Tolosa. They were subsequently launched into gastronomic orbit by a talented generation of new Basque cooks who, understanding how well

OPPOSITE: (LEFT TO RIGHT) *PIQUILLO* PEPPERS IN THE FIELD AND IN THE TIN. ABOVE: FIELD OF *PIQUILLO* PEPPERS NEAR LODOSA

they hold their shape even when cooked, stuffed them with foie gras, squid, crab, pork, black pudding, salt cod, hake and more. In only twenty years the yield multiplied thirty-fold, and *piquillo* peppers became a modern Spanish classic.

Today, only a modest amount of other peppers are grown, and hung out to dry in ruby-red festoons from balconies. The best *piquillo* seeds are reserved from year to year, and the seedlings are planted out in May, irrigated, fertilized and hoed during the spring and summer. During harvesting, from September to November, the ripe peppers must be carefully picked in order not to break the stem, which is held by a clip as they pass through the commercial roasting ovens.

Privately, some locals still roast their peppers over coals in old-fashioned tin drums, rather like hot chestnuts, turning the peppers at the top until they fall into the bottom part. A few artisan producers such as the Perón family, who also grow their own peppers (slogan: *'De la mata, a la lata* – from the plant to the tin), use wood-fired ovens. Pyrenean beech, which gives off an intense heat and sweet, smoky flavour, is brought down from the mountains along the Camino de Santiago.

At the larger Cooperativa del Campo de Lodosa, they switched to butane gas a few years ago in order to get a more uniform product. However, as they explained, it is the flame, not the heat, that is the crucial factor; the skin must be scorched for easy peeling, but the flesh has to remain firm. After roasting, while still hot, the peppers are individually hand-skinned using a cloth and a small knife, cored and seeded. Then they are carefully trimmed so that they remain whole and unbroken, and packed tightly in herringbone layers in cans and jars, without ever coming into contact with either water or brine. No seasoning is needed; they are simply peppers in their own natural juice.

Success brings its own share of problems: many canned peppers are marketed as *piquillo* peppers, even though their provenance and production methods are somewhat doubtful. Only those peppers with the tightly controlled D.O. Lodosa label are guaranteed to have been grown in the region, from the correct variety, and to have been produced using a basic artisan process that has changed over the years only in degree of technology.

Cayo Martínez, of Viuda de Cayo, showed me round the huge state-of-the-art factory founded by his grandmother in Mendavia, one of the towns in the growing region. His seventy-five-year-old mother still worked from dawn to dusk on the production line alongside the Andalucian seasonal workers ('but she's the one who still gives all the orders!'). Cayo had pioneered the use of a new system of traceability: 'I can tell from the label which part of the field the pepper came from – now that's traceability!' Then, holding up exhibits A and B, as in a court of law, he explained: 'Look, those peppers are not D.O. – they're watery, without any of the *piquillo's* natural oils, smokey aroma, intensity of flavour or even characteristic flecks of charred skin. Yes, we produce them for certain customers, and they are cheaper, but they're nothing like the real thing. Put them side by side, and you can easily tell the difference.'

The *Ribera*, the fertile, gently rolling region found to the north of the Ebro is famous for vines, horticulture and the preserving skills of the local peple: at other times of the year, the factories are busy canning and bottling asparagus, artichokes, peaches, *pochas* (green beans), cardoons, mushrooms and more. In the window of the Péron factory there are display-only jars of asparagus the thickness of a baby's arm and onions the size of small rocks, but to my mind it is the ruby red pepper that is the jewel in the crown of Navarre.

ABOVE: *PIQUILLO* PEPPERS READY TO SHIP. OPPOSITE: PÉRON FACTORY, LODOSA

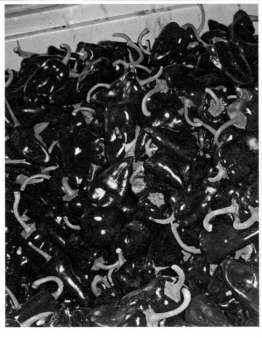

Piquillo Peppers with Ham and Scrambled Egg

SERVES 1

Oil and butter (or fresh lard)

1 shallot, finely chopped

1 medium garlic clove, finely chopped

2 piquillo peppers, cut into thin strips

2 slices *jamón serrano* (or more if wished)

2 eggs, beaten with 15 g/½ oz chopped fresh parsley

Salt and black pepper

Toasted country bread (for serving)

Heat a little oil and butter in a frying pan or, better still, a heatproof earthenware dish, and gently fry the shallot and garlic until light gold. Add the peppers and ham, and cook for another few minutes.

Pour the eggs into the pan, season, and stir until they just start to set. They should not be overcooked. Top, if wished, with extra strips of grilled *jamón*, and serve with toasted country bread.

Traditional *Pimientos del Piquillo de Lodosa*

The Martínez family own the elegant La Galera restaurant and *sidrería* in Mendavia, where the starters include platters of velvety tinned white asparagus drizzled with their own olive oil, baby leeks, and deep-fried Tudela artichokes wrapped in ham. Main course chargrilled baby lamb chops are served with *piquillo* peppers, flanking the meat like miniature bullfighters' capes. As the entire table explained to me, all you have to do is turn the peppers into a frying pan, add a little olive oil, sliced garlic, sea salt and a pinch of sugar, and cook over a very low heat for 10 minutes, gently shaking the pan from time to time.

NOTE: A 425 g/15 oz tin will contain approximately 18–20 peppers.

LEFT: *PIQUILLO* PEPPERS WITH HAM AND SCRAMBLED EGG

ABOVE: PEPPERS DRYING IN THE SUN, LODOSA

Stuffed *Piquillo* Peppers with Vegetables and Blue Cheese Sauce

For best results, use an earthenware dish that can be heated on the top of the stove (with a diffuser mat, if necessary).

SERVES 4

425 g/ a 15 oz tin of *piquillo* peppers	1 green pepper, finely chopped
125 ml/4 fl oz olive oil	1 large tomato, skinned, seeded and finely chopped
1 medium onion, finely chopped	150 ml/5 fl oz single cream
1 medium courgette, finely chopped	100 g/3½ oz Spanish blue cheese, such as Cabrales, crumbled
1 leek, finely chopped	
1 large carrot, finely chopped	Sherry vinegar
1 stick of celery, finely chopped	Salt and black pepper

Carefully empty the contents of the tin, including any natural juices, into a bowl.

Heat the oil in a large pan and add the vegetables. Cover, lower the heat and cook gently until the vegetables are soft. Season with salt and pepper, turn up the heat, and cook uncovered for a few minutes to evaporate any excess liquid. Remove from the heat.

When the vegetable filling is cool enough to handle, use a teaspoon to stuff each pepper with some of the mixture. This is slightly tricky, as the peppers are slippery to handle, but not difficult. Cup each one in your hand, carefully squeezing it open, trying not to tear the pepper as you work. If you like, you can close the top of each pepper with a toothpick to stop the filling leaking out (remove the toothpicks before serving). Pack into a heatproof earthenware dish just large enough to hold the peppers closely together and drizzle with any juices left in the bowl.

Mix the cream and crumbled cheese in a saucepan and heat gently, seasoning with black pepper and a splash of sherry vinegar. Pour half this sauce over the peppers.

Warm the peppers gently over a low heat. Serve with the remaining sauce on the side.

Hake with *Piquillo* Pepper Sauce

The Bay of Biscay produces some of the finest hake, and it is a prized fish throughout northern Spain. Some cooks like to add to the dramatic colours of the dish with slices of cooked carrot, but personally I think this verges on Marbella sunset.

SERVES 4

FOR THE SAUCE:	
3–4 tablespoons olive oil	Salt
1 onion, chopped	4 hake steaks, seasoned with salt
2 garlic cloves, chopped	4 tablespoons olive oil
2 *piquillo* peppers, cut into strips	Juice of 1 lemon
The white part of a leek, sliced	2 *piquillo* peppers, cut into strips
3 large ripe tomatoes, peeled, seeded and chopped	Chopped fresh parsley (optional)
50ml/2 fl oz white wine	

To make the sauce, heat the oil in a frying pan and slowly fry the onions for about 10 minutes, until they start to soften. Add the garlic and when the aroma arises add the peppers and leek. Stir in the tomatoes, then the wine. Add salt, to taste, and simmer for 10–15 minutes until soft and thick. Cool slightly, and purée the sauce. (If wished, the sauce can be made in advance.)

Place the fish in a heatproof dish and drizzle with olive oil and lemon juice. Either cook on top of the stove, on a medium heat, shaking the dish gently from time to time, or bake in a preheated oven (180°C/350°F/Gas Mark 4) for 15–20 minutes, basting occasionally.

Reheat the sauce while the fish is cooking. You can add any juices from the fish to the sauce for extra flavour.

Serve the fish topped with the sauce and criss-crossed with strips of *piquillo* pepper and sprinkled with parsley.

RIGHT: HAKE WITH *PIQUILLO* PEPPER SAUCE

TENERIFE: bananas

bananarama

Size isn't everything, as the amply endowed actress says to the little old man she meets in the elevator, half-hidden under a bunch of unnaturally large, rigid yellow fruit. She points instead to her own bunch of cute little speckled bananas – *plátanos de Canarias*. Cut to the expression on the old man's face. *¡Caramba!*

The TV commercial may have been none too subtle but it made a point: on the one hand, there is the oversized 'dollar banana', with its waxy, embalmed, sickly lemon colour, blade-sharp edges, thick rubbery skin and bland fibrous flesh, and on the other, a golden, sweet and fragrant little euro-banana with soft curves and creamy, rich fruit. What it does not mention is the hard economic realities of the marketplace. In the world banana wars, this little gem of a fruit has had to fight to stay in business; only

by intervention and subsidies has the Canary banana industry been able to stand up to the low-priced fruit that has flooded the market from the large growers in Latin and South America. Helped, also, by the discernment of Spanish shoppers, who can still tell a decent banana from a gun-in-your-pocket impostor.

There is a degree of irony in the story, not lost on the local growers, who probably wish the sixteenth-century *conquistadores* and priests had never taken the banana plant to Latin America in the first place. Bananas were first introduced to the Canaries in the fifteenth century by the Portuguese, but remained an exotic ornamental shrub until the nineteenth century when commercial planting began after the failure of the sugar cane, wine and cochineal trade. It was pioneered by English companies, such as Fyffes, who identified suitable sites on the northern side of the island where they could plant the dwarf

OPPOSITE: (LEFT TO RIGHT) BANANAS WRAPPED FOR TRANSPORT; BANANAS ON SALE, MALÁGA MARKET; BANANA PLANTATION NEAR GARACHICO. ABOVE: BANANA PLANTATION

Musa cavendishii, imported from Indochina. The British merchant fleet was able to transport this healthy new gourmet fruit swiftly to Canary Wharf in London, and by the 1930s so much fruit was sent to Germany and France that Josephine Baker raised bourgeois eyebrows when she sported an erotic banana skirt.

This happy state of affairs was cruelly disrupted in turn by the First World War, the Wall Street Crash, the Spanish Civil War and the Second World War, followed by massive migration until tourism arrived to transform the islands' economies. By the 1960s, trade had recovered sufficiently that almost half the crop was exported again, mainly to the UK. Then, another blow: advances in transatlantic shipping, the introduction of refrigerated technology and clever marketing paved the way for the invasion of the multinational 'dollar banana'. Not only that, but their production costs – starvation wages, according to Canary producers – were far lower. Nonetheless, one could also argue that competition has made the local industry improve product quality and yield, as well as lead the way in methods of cleaning, packing, transportation and high-tech traceability.

Bananas remain the leading crop of the Canary Islands, a scattering of volcanic islands just above the Tropic of Cancer: legend has it that they are part of the lost continent of Atlantis. A sovereign part of Spain, yet with an identity all their own, they once formed the western edge of the known world. Bananas are grown throughout the archipelago, but the commercial centre is Tenerife, an island of two halves, divided by more than the volcanic peak of Mount Teide, the legendary home of Guayota, the 'Evil One', according to the folk legends of the *guanches*, the indigenous people of the islands.

The southern part of Tenerife is Time-Share Central, an arid and dull stretch of coast that has been scarred by ugly developments, garish bars and soulless resorts. The banana plantations, largely covered with net or plastic sheeting for wind protection, are as unattractive as the interminable, ticky-tacky boxes of holiday homes. Yet only a short (albeit white-knuckle) drive away there are Wagnerian mountains, lunar landscapes, deep and dizzy gorges, prehistoric forests, unspoilt villages, tropical gardens, living fossil dragon trees, and charming Canarian houses. Plus a renewed sense of self-belief and island pride that takes the form of the thrilling white arc of the new Auditorium designed by Santiago Calatrava in the capital, Santa Cruz.

In the north, the Mardi Gras colours of Tenerife are intense in the bright island light: black sand and golden fruit, brick red earth and navy blue breakers with lacy cream foam where the waves dissolve upon the rocks. Fluorescent orange and purple flowers of science-fiction intensity interrupt the vivid green scrub, and the snows of Mount Teide's summit are an uncompromising streak of white against the cloudless sky.

Here the vertiginous terraces of bananas, potatoes, tomatoes, avocados and mangoes planted around sugar-cube houses are a testimony to hard work and native grit, a mulish obstinacy to carve out a living from every available nook, cranny and patch of land, as well as a naturally anarchic attitude towards

ABOVE: 1930S FRENCH BANANA POSTER. RIGHT: (LEFT TO RIGHT) DRAGON TREE; SWIMMING POOL, PUERTO DE LA CRUZ

planning regulations. Unlike the immense agro-industrial banana plantations of Ecuador, Tenerife remains an island of family farms, each plot divided and subdivided down the generations. As a result, the bananas are grown with horticultural care, and a number of farmers still have a flock of local sheep that graze on the banana leaves, their manure used for compost. The plantations face the sea, in the same way that the families of poor emigrants once patiently waited at lookout points for their return from the New World. A poignant, perennial story of economic migrancy that is played out daily in one the most popular dishes of the islands, *arroz a la cubana*, made with fried eggs, white rice, tomato sauce and fried bananas.

It all begins, however, with a good banana. The first thing I learnt was that the main variety is the Pequeña Enana or Small Dwarf, which makes it sound like a character in a fairy-tale. It grows well in the Canaries, because its short stature allows it to survive the trade winds. Although these winds provide the blissful cool breezes that make Tenerife a summer oasis for Spaniards escaping the mainland heat, they can also on occasion whip through the fragile leaves of the banana plant, tearing them to ragged fringes.

In a plantation near the old banana-boat port of Garachico, squeezed between the mountains and the unlimited horizons of the Atlantic Ocean, I saw how windbreaks protected the trees from both wind and salt spray, and how wooden crutches were used to prop the massive clusters of fruit, like green chandeliers, away from the main stem. Sometimes the growing bunches were wrapped in perforated plastic bags to protect the delicate skin. The work is laborious; the terrain does not permit mechanization.

Water is the biggest, and most expensive, problem, and every plant requires over 20 litres a day to ripen just one kilo of fruit. Rainfall is insufficient, so this can only be achieved with artificial irrigation, and the plantations are criss-crossed with pipes, pumping water from a remarkable, extensive complex of underground wells mined from deep under Mount Teide, as well as from with newer reservoirs.

The quality of the Canary banana, however, is also down to freshness and timing. Even though they are still shipped by sea, the journey is far quicker to their destination markets than those from Latin and South America. The latter have to be cut while still green and undeveloped in order to endure many weeks, sometimes months, of refrigerated transport and artificial ripening. Without going into brain-numbing detail about starches and sugar conversion, even my simple, non-scientific mind can grasp the point that if the Canary banana takes only two or three days to reach the market, it can be cut at the closest point possible to maturity, when it is nicely fattened up, filling its skin like a plump little sausage, and just before its sweetest, ripest, balanced best.

The main drawback is that the peel is far more sensitive to crude handling. No slinging a great bunch in the back of a truck or on open pallets for these delicate little thin-skinned Canaries, as happens with their tough-as-nails South American cousins. Kid-glove care is taken to prevent bruising at every point in the chain; this includes swaddling the bananas in padded blankets and quilting, and meticulously stacking them in protective boxes. Old photographs show how women were traditionally employed to

ABOVE: GARACHICO.

grade and pack the bananas because of their lightness of touch, packing them in hay or pine leaves instead of today's bubble wrap. These pretty girls were testimony to the health-giving properties of bananas, carrying 30-kilo bunches as if they were a stack of hatboxes and they were about to run up Mount Teide with them.

Contrary to modern misinformation, the Canary banana is at its prime of perfect quality and ripeness when the golden skin takes on a characteristic scattering of dark freckles, but Island cooks are expert in judging firmness simply by appearance and fragrance. At the Michelin-starred Mesón El Drago in Tegueste, Carlos Gamonal ripens his own *plátanos* on the stem by hanging them in the middle of the restaurant from a large hook over an ancient wooden press laden with an array of beautiful, unpasteurized local cheese. Carlos has followed in the footsteps of this father, also a renowned chef, and his brother works alongside him in the kitchen.

His menu is structured on clever reinterpretations of traditional dishes, a commitment to local ingredients and a philosophy (indeed, poetry) that derives from his island roots: 'How can you limit gastronomy in a place where the sky is endless, where the sea defines your world, where the colours are like a thousand rainbows, where the smell of the fruits of the earth are in the very air we breathe. I want to show how all these things can be concentrated within the perimeter of a white plate on the table. The Canary banana is very special, and very adaptable. When I cook them with meat or fish, I have to add some lemon or vinegar to balance the sweetness, but when I'm developing a recipe and need something sweet, my first thought is always of the banana. It is a fruit that is a real spur to creativity in the kitchen.'

I carried a bunch of Canary bananas back to England with me. When I opened my bag, my kitchen filled with a heady fragrance that brought a tantalizing memory of a small, friendly island floating off the coast of Africa. Tenerife, a historical staging post and culinary crossroads between so many worlds, where each banana tastes like a luscious fruit cocktail: strawberries, pineapple, peaches. As the TV advert said, they're simply *insustituible*.

ABOVE: (LEFT TO RIGHT) BEACH, PUERTO DE LA CRUZ; BANANA PLANTATION ON THE SLOPES OF MOUNT TEIDE

Banana Tart with Rum and Raisins

SERVE 6-8

400 g/14 oz sweet shortcrust pastry

1 large egg white, lightly beaten

4 soft bananas (to make about 300 g/10½ oz when peeled), sliced and sprinkled with the juice of half a lemon

100 g/3½ oz raisins, presoaked in 30 ml/1 fl oz rum

50 g/1¾ oz lightly toasted, slivered almonds

1 whole large egg

2 large egg yolks

75 ml/3 fl oz double cream

100 g/3½ oz caster sugar

Zest of 1 lemon

1 teaspoon ground cinnamon

Preheat the oven to 200°C/400°F/Gas Mark 6.

Line a 25 cm/10 inch loose-bottomed, metal flan tin with the pastry. Bake blind in the preheated oven for 10 minutes, then remove from the oven and brush the surface of the pastry with some of the lightly beaten egg white. Lower the heat to 180°C/350°F/Gas Mark 4 and bake for another 5 minutes.

Remove from the oven and arrange the bananas over the pastry, sprinkling with the raisins and almonds. Lower the oven temperature to 160C/325F/Gas Mark 3.

Beat the whole egg, egg yolks, cream, sugar, lemon zest and cinnamon. Pour over the fruit, and return to the oven for 20–25 minutes until set. Serve at room temperature.

Little Banana and Cinnamon Pancakes

These are also delicious served with vanilla ice cream.

MAKES ABOUT 24

6 ripe bananas, peeled and mashed

4 tablespoons flour, sifted with 1 teaspoon baking powder

Zest of 1 lemon

2 large eggs, separated

1 teaspoon cinnamon

50 ml/2 fl oz milk

Salt

Oil, for frying

Icing sugar

Blend the bananas with the flour and baking powder, lemon zest, egg yolks, cinnamon, milk and a pinch of salt to make a fairly thick batter. Set aside to rest for 30 minutes.

Just before you're ready to fry the pancakes, beat the egg whites until stiff and fold into the banana mixture. Heat enough oil to cover the bottom of a frying pan. Drop spoonfuls of the batter into the oil and fry until brown on both sides.

Drain on kitchen paper and sprinkle with icing sugar.

ABOVE: PLAYGROUND, PUERTO DE LA CRUZ

LEFT: BANANA TART WITH RUM AND RAISINS

Tropical Banana Cake

The exotic fruit can be replaced by any variety, but these reflect the magnificent range grown in the Canary Islands, many of which were originally natives of other continents but which flourish in the glorious subtropical climate.

SERVES 4–6

4 eggs, separated
100 g/3½ oz sugar
25 g/1 oz flour, sifted with
 ½ teaspoon baking powder
100 g/3½ oz ground almonds
50 g/1¾ oz flaked almonds
Zest of 1 lemon
Butter
1 small banana, plus assorted
 sliced fruit such as mango,
 guava, pineapple and kiwi
 (to give a total of about
 500 g/1 lb 2 oz)
Whipped cream (optional)

FOR THE SYRUP:
200 g/7 oz sugar
100 ml/3½ oz lemon juice
100 ml/3½ oz orange juice
1–2 tablespoons banana liqueur
 (optional)

Preheat the oven to 180°C/350°F/Gas Mark 5.

Whisk the egg yolks with the sugar until foamy. Mix in the flour and baking powder, ground and flaked almonds, and lemon zest. Whip the egg whites with a pinch of salt until they just start to form snowy peaks. Gently but thoroughly fold the whipped egg whites into the cake mixture.

Turn into a well-buttered shallow cake tin (20 cm/8 inches) or ring mould (23 cm/9 inches) and bake for 20–30 minutes until golden. Leave to cool before turning out on to a serving dish.

To make the syrup, slowly heat the sugar and fruit juice, stirring frequently. When it starts to boil, cook for a few more minutes. Remove from the heat and add the liqueur, if using. Leave to cool.

Slice the banana and mix with the other fruit. Top or fill the sponge cake with the fruit, and pour the syrup over fruit and cake. Leave for at least 10 minutes for the cake to absorb some of the syrup, then serve with whipped cream.

Baked Bananas with Ginger Cream and Coconut Sorbet

A recipe based on one from Laly Carayon, chef-proprietor of the peaceful San Roque Hotel in Garachico, a beautifully restored seventeenth-century manor house that she and her husband have transformed into a sophisticated small hotel filled with contemporary art and style. If you like, you can add shard of coconut brittle or some slices of fresh mango for extra colour.

SERVES 6

FOR THE GINGER CREAM:
1 litre/1¾ pints cream
50 g/1¾ oz finely diced stem
 ginger in syrup (or use fresh
 ginger, peeled and sliced and
 drain before cooling)
12 egg yolks
125 g/4½ oz sugar

4 gelatine leaves, soaked in cold
 water
1 small, ripe banana per person,
 cut in half lengthways
2 teaspoons sugar per banana
1 teaspoon cream per banana
Lime juice

Put the cream into a pan with the ginger and heat until almost boiling; take off the heat and leave to infuse for 5 minutes.

Beat the eggs and sugar and add to the cream. Place over a very low heat, stirring constantly, for several minutes, but take care not to let the mixture boil. Stir in the dissolved gelatine, and pour the mixture into small individual pots. Set aside to cool, and refrigerate.

Heat the sugar with a few drops of water until it starts to caramelize, and mix with the cream and a squeeze of lime juice. Arrange the bananas in a heatproof dish, and pour over the creamy syrup. Put under the grill briefly and set aside.

Remove the ginger cream from the fridge and stir each pot. Arrange the bananas on top (cut smaller, if wished) and serve with a scoop of sorbet.

(To make coconut sorbet, combine 250 ml/9 fl oz of sweetened coconut milk with 500 ml/18 fl oz water and the zest of 1 lime, and freeze in an ice cream machine according to the manufacturer's instructions. Add a splash of rum, if wished.)

RIGHT: TROPICAL BANANA CAKE

VALENCIA: oranges

oranges are the only fruit

The rain in Spain was falling mainly on my head. In the distance, the towers and turrets of the city of Valencia, the great city of El Cid, were barely visible; the glossy domes of the new City of Arts and Sciences, a damp blur. Somewhere to my right were the waters of the marshy, coastal lake of Albufera, known for its ricefields. In front, the Mediterranean was as grey as the heart of a stone saint. I was in the heart of the great orange garden of Spain, and about to have all romantic notions of golden fruit and amorous sheiks dispelled from my mind. Spain is the largest exporter of oranges in the world, and citrus fruit is a modern agribusiness; producers, packers, merchants and exporters have to be up-to-date and competitive with planting and new varieties designed to stretch the season, ensure consistent supply and

minimize the time between tree and table. Yet all the high-tech research labs, warehouse sophistication, trading exchanges and transport logistics still depend – *al fondo* – on two, age-old things: Nature and Man.

'We need the rain. It's the end of February and we've had a very dry winter,' explained José Vincente, field manager for Frutsol. 'The pickers also welcome it. Oranges have to be fully ripe when picked and need gentle handling; they still haven't invented a machine to do the job. But the pickers can't work in a downpour – the trees close in on themselves, like people huddling from the rain, and are so wet they'd drown the pickers. More importantly, once picked the fruit must not get wet or it will rot. So the pickers get a day off, and can spend it in the bar instead!' The newly washed leaves were dark and glossy, each branch heavy with acid-sweet Navelates. Yellow wildflowers, brought out by the rain, filled the spaces

OPPOSITE: (LEFT TO RIGHT) ORANGES, NEAR VALENCIA; ORANGE TREES, VALENCIA CITY CENTRE.
ABOVE: ORANGE GROVE NEAR VALENCIA

between the trees; the air reflected the rich, earthy aroma of the soil. A good, natural smell, though I wanted to be there in April, when the trees are as pretty as spring brides, and the intense perfume of the blossom as intoxicating as the local *Agua de Valencia*, a lethal brew of orange juice, Cava and brandy. They say that at one time sailors could smell the scent of the Valencian orange blossom drifting out to sea.

José, an engaging and lively character, had worked in the citrus industry all his life. What was his favourite season, I asked? 'This one. When I see all those oranges, I think of all the money it brings to my pocket!' It was more than a quip; almost everyone here has a vested interest in the citrus groves. Historically, inheritance laws divided the land between the children of farmers, and as a result nearly every family owns a grove somewhere, even if they no longer live in the countryside themselves. Most plots are small, although the local Lladró and Porcelanosa families are also some of the largest landowners. One way or the other, a poor harvest, bad weather or falling prices affects everyone.

Valencia. Oranges. Oranges. Valencia. The association is inescapable. Walking through the sensual, slightly oriental streets and squares of the city that was once called the Queen of the Levante, it is easy to understand why orange trees were considered one of three essential components of Moorish garden design, along with multi-coloured tiles and ornamental fountains. There are trees in small gardens, and orange motif mosaics on the splendid *modernista* railway station and the façade of the Colón market.

A glass of freshly picked and squeezed juice served with a sachet of sugar is a popular dessert throughout Spain, especially early in the year when the fruits of winter are a reminder of the sun. As Nicolás Belmonte Martínez, director of Intercitrus, reflected: 'Nature is wise. Oranges and mandarins are seasonal, full of vitamin C, good for winter colds. Of course, there is an element of habit, but I think there is also a genetic impulse that explains why we are so drawn to citrus fruit in winter. Citrus consumption has always been higher in cold weather, but now we are losing that seasonal tradition as fruit is easily available all year round.'

Bitter oranges, still grown for British marmalade around Seville, arrived with the Arabs, some two centuries before the returning Crusaders brought the first specimens to Sicily and Italy from the Near East. They were grown for their medicinal and aesthetic qualities, sometimes compared to glowing embers or 'cheeks glimpsed through green curtains of covered litters' In the sixteenth century the Portuguese introduced sweet oranges from China: the phrase is echoed in a rather archaic Spanish expression that means an impossible dream. Even now, the words satsuma and mandarin echo that exotic, oriental origin. In 1781 a local priest planted the first commercial orange grove in Valencia. It was an astute move; the coastal plains to the north and south provided a frost-free microclimate that proved a perfect home for the fruit, helped by a sophisticated irrigation system inherited from the Arabs, without which the *huerta* would be as parched as the plains of Castile. Today, limited only by sea and a range of angular mountains, an army of groves occupies every available inch; banners of brilliant orange and baize-green as far as the eye can see.

The story of this beautiful fruit is documented in the fascinating Museu de la Taronja (Valencian for Orange Museum), housed in a beautiful old house in Burriana, south of Castellón. The Museum is a tribute to the vision of Vicente Abad García, a quietly spoken agricultural engineer and historian whose gentle manners cloak a life-long love affair with oranges. Born in Burriana, once one of the Mediterranean

ABOVE: CAFÉ SOCIETY, VALENCIA. OPPOSITE: (TOP) VALENCIA MARKET; (LEFT) VALENCIA CATHEDRAL; (RIGHT) CRATE OF ORANGES, VALENCIA

ports where the fruit was loaded on to ships bound for northern Europe, he dryly joked that the only things the old men used to talk about in the town when he was growing up were: 'Oranges, football and women! That's why I left for Madrid.'

Trade quickly developed in the nineteenth century, spurred on by a series of crises in the silk, hemp and wine industries. The Valencians, a trading people since Phoenician times, soon took advantage of the export opportunities offered by the growth of steamship navigation combined with an increased demand in the industrialized countries of Europe for fresh fruit; the rapid spread of the orange groves changed the landscape for ever. Today, the main commercial imperative is for good-looking, easy-peeling, no-seed fruit, but at one time an astonishing 5,000 varieties were recorded. In the early twentieth century the Washington Navel, round as a Belisha beacon, was introduced; so-called because of its visible 'navel' at the point where the blossom appears. Its descendants, such as Navelina and Navelate, now make up the majority of the crop, along with the 'white group', Salustiana and Valencia Late, and blood oranges such as Sanguinelli and Sanguina, although nearly as many small oranges, especially clementines, are now grown as their big brother oranges.

Once every child's Christmas stocking in Britain would conceal an unimaginably exotic scented tangerine, far sweeter in my mind than most sharp little clementines. This memory of Christmas Past, when the finest Spanish oranges would arrive individually wrapped, was also conjured up in the wonderful display in the Museum of silk paper wrappings and orange-crate labels. In the first half of the last century,

ABOVE: (LEFT TO RIGHT) JOSÉ SLICING OPEN AN ORANGE; ORANGES, VALENCIA MARKET.
OPPOSITE: VALENCIA MARKET

some of the most talented artists in Valencia worked as graphic designers in the citrus industry, and the polychromatic art nouveau and art deco labels are decorative, exuberant and witty, always eye-catching if sometimes a touch bizarre. Vicente pointed out a label from his family's firm, The Wireless Brand, showing an old-fashioned radio with all stations calling 'Eat More Fruit' and oranges coming out of the box labelled Liverpool, London, Glasgow and Manchester. This link between fruit and art continues today in the prestigious annual photographic competition sponsored by the citrus industry.

Back to the future. The dynamics of the modern business world mean increasing competition from both other countries and other regions of Spain with more space, lower costs and higher margins. Citrus groves are also being dug up to provide land for new golf courses and holiday homes, but Vicente was positive, 'Yes, we have challenges, but we also have 200 years of experience, and a Research Institute that continues to push the boundaries forward. But everything has its season, and if you get fruit too early on to the market it can affect the quality. Supermarkets are also guilty of trying to drive the price downwards all the time, so they end up with poor fruit. Too many people around the world think that an orange is an orange is an orange, but no housewife in Valencia will buy oranges ready-packed from the supermarket, they want to feel and weigh them by hand. I always say that you should never ask the shopper to buy an orange that you wouldn't eat yourself if given it for free. I know that when they taste them, people are always surprised at the quality of oranges from Valencia. We don't practise agriculture here; essentially, we are still gardeners.'

In the silence of the orange grove, José pulled out his pocket knife and slit open an orange, luminous as a still life by Zurbarán, to reveal the dripping, brilliant flesh. Never mind the variety, he said. The best fruit is the one you eat straight from the tree.

Toasted Bread with Garlic and Orange

Although it sounds unlikely, this variation on a theme of bread and oil works brilliantly. It uses bitter Seville oranges, and is based on a recipe from the Málaga region, published in 1957 by Elizabeth Cass in *Spanish Cooking*. She adds that in Estepona it is known as *gazpacho colorado*. Today, you could call it *tosta del sol*.

PER PERSON – OR, AT LEAST, ONE SLICE OF BREAD

1 large garlic clove

Chilli pepper flakes

3 tablespoons Seville orange juice (or 2 tablespoons sweet orange juice and 1 tablespoon lemon juice)

1 tablespoon olive oil

1 thick slice of country or sourdough bread

Salt and black pepper

Preheat the oven to 180°C/350°F/Gas Mark 4.

Put the peeled garlic into a mortar with a little salt, and pound to a paste. Add a few grinds of chilli pepper flakes (from a mill is best) and black pepper. Stir in the orange juice and the oil.

Spread the mixture over the bread and place on a lightly oiled baking tray. Bake for 5–10 minutes (your nose will tell you when it's ready), and serve straight away.

Orange and Avocado Salad

Although this recipe comes from the Canary Islands, the use of citrus juice to dress salads dates from Moorish times.

SERVES 4

3–4 avocados, depending on size

Lemon juice

3 oranges, peeled and segmented

3 Little Gem lettuces or lettuce hearts, shredded

FOR THE DRESSING:

1 orange, juiced

1 large egg yolk

2 tablespoons mustard

6 tablespoons olive oil

Salt and black pepper

Peel, stone and slice the avocados and sprinkle with lemon juice.

Whisk the orange juice, egg yolk, mustard, olive oil and seasoning until thick and opaque.

Arrange the avocados, orange segments and shredded lettuce in a serving bowl. Drizzle with the dressing (as much as feels right to you) and toss gently before serving.

ABOVE: MOSAIC, VALENCIA RAILWAY STATION

RIGHT: ORANGE AND AVOCADO SALAD

Hake in Orange and Saffron Sauce

A dish so colourful you almost need your sunglasses. It can also be made with grouper, bass or other white fish.

SERVES 4

4 tablespoons olive oil

4 hake steaks or fillets, sprinkled with salt

2 garlic cloves, finely chopped

2 tablespoons capers

25 g/1 oz fresh mint or parsley, finely chopped

Pinch of crushed chilli pepper (optional)

1 teaspoon cornflour or arrowroot

Juice of 2 oranges

Juice of 1 lemon

A pinch of saffron filaments, lightly crushed and soaked in a little hot water

Heat the oil in a frying pan and lightly brown the fish on both sides. Remove from the pan with a spatula and place in a heatproof dish.

Add the garlic to the oil and fry briefly. When golden, stir in the capers, mint or parsley and crushed chilli pepper, if using, and spread this mixture over the fish.

Dissolve the cornflour in the orange and lemon juice, stir in the saffron, and add the liquid to the dish. Cook on a low heat on top of the stove for 10 minutes, shaking the dish gently from time to time. Serve straight from the dish.

Duck with Orange Sauce

This recipe is based on a recipe in *La Taronja*, a fund-raising booklet written in Valencian, produced by the parents and children of a school in La Safor. It stars two of the most famous ingredients of the region: oranges (*¡claro!*), and duck from La Albufera.

SERVES 4

1 tablespoon oil

1 whole duck, 2.5 kg–3 kg/5–6 lb

1 onion, finely chopped

1 tablespoon tomato purée

150 ml/5 fl oz water

75 ml/3 fl oz white wine

Juice of 1 orange

Juice of 1 lemon

3 teaspoons sugar

3 teaspoons sherry vinegar

1 tsp flour

125 ml/4 fl oz orange liqueur

3 large oranges, segmented, with pith and membrane removed.

Salt and ground pepper

Preheat the oven to 220°C/425°F/Gas Mark 7.

Season the duck and roast in the preheated oven for 20 minutes, then turn the heat down to 180°C/350°F/Gas Mark 4. Roast for a total of 20 minutes per 500 g/1 lb 2 oz (calculating the total cooking time from when the bird first goes into the oven). Once cooked, pour off the excess fat and leave the duck to rest in a warm place for 30 minutes.

Halfway through the cooking time, heat the oil in a saucepan and gently soften the onion for at least 10 minutes. When it turns translucent, add the tomato purée, water and wine. Bring to the boil, and simmer for 10 minutes.

Add the orange and lemon juice, and simmer for another 10 minutes. Dissolve the sugar in the vinegar, and add to the sauce. Season, and simmer for 5 minutes.

Stir the flour into the liqueur, and add to the sauce. Stir in the orange segments, simmer for 5 minutes, and serve with the duck.

Delicias

Almond and chocolate 'delights'. An understatement!

MAKES 24

100 g/3½ oz plain chocolate (around 70% cocoa content)

25 g/1 oz butter

1 tablespoon single cream or creamy milk

100 g/3½ oz icing sugar

4 tablespoons orange juice

200 g/7 oz ground almonds

Break the chocolate into chunks and melt it with the butter and milk until it forms a thick coating sauce. You can either do this in a bain-marie or in the microwave (stirring halfway through).

Dissolve the icing sugar in the orange juice, and add the ground almonds. Mix until the paste feels slightly sticky and starts to hold together in clumps. Add a little more juice, if necessary.

Pinch off small pieces and use your hands to shape, squeeze and roll them into small, smooth balls. Dip each one in the chocolate sauce until well coated (hands are also best for this, aided perhaps by a spoon, so expect sticky fingers). Arrange on a baking sheet covered with greaseproof or parchment paper, and chill for at least an hour.

Place each one in a ruffled paper case and serve with strong black coffee.

LEFT: HAKE IN ORANGE AND SAFFRON SAUCE

Index

Page numbers in **bold** refer to feature text, page numbers in *italic* refer to photographs

Amongst the many people that helped me research this book, I would like to thank the following:

ARAGON: Juan Barbacil Pérez; Juan Baseda; Carlos Estevan Martínez; Jesus Carceller Prats
ASTURIAS: Soledad F. Lafuente
BASQUE COUNTRY: Elena Ruiz de Azua Esturo
CANTABRIA: Diego Velasco Ballesteros; Kiko Martínez Nates
CASTILE LA MANCHA: Francisco J. Alfaro Ponce; the Dehesa de Los Llanos; Pedro Condés Torrres
CASTILE-LEON: Eloy Vaquero Hernández
CASTILE-MADRID: Zacarias Merinero
CATALONIA: Antonio Borrás; David Antolín Velasco
EXTREMADURA: Bonifacio Sánchez Cruz; Julia Paz Garcia
GALICIA: Maria Dolores Loureda
LA RIOJA: Sixto Cabezon
MAJORCA: Luis Miguel Herrero; Hotel Dalt Murada, Palma and the Sancho family; Monika Potthast of the Balearic Tourist Board
MALAGA: Javier Aranda Bautista; Maria Utrera of the Costa del Sol Tourist Board; Hotel California, Malaga
MURCIA: José María García Soto; María Jesús Gil Cantos of the Murcia Tourist Board; Hotel NH Rincon de Pepe, Murcia
NAVARRE: Isabel Peñaranda González-Llanos
TENERIFE: Enrique Alvarez Sanfiel; Susie Fairfax; Tenerife Tourism; Hotel Mirador Suites Turquesa, Puerto de la Cruz
VALENCIA: Salvador Maroto

I am also indebted to the following for their invaluable support and advice:

María José Sevilla and Celia Resel of Foods From Spain, London; Pamela Phillips and Manuel Hierro; Kepa González of the Instituto Cervantes, Manchester; Nori del Arco of the Spanish Tourist Board, London; Monarch Scheduled Airlines; Richard Burt, Little Spain; agapes.com; Brindisa Spanish Foods, London

My thanks, also to Michele Barlow, Duncan Poyser and Emma Sturgess for their willingness to test recipes; to Peter Cassidy, Jacque Malouf and Alison Fenton for making the book look beautiful; to Katey Day for her patience and encouragement; and to my agent Michael Alcock for all his support. Thanks, as ever, to family and friends and, above all, to the people of Spain for their unfailing kindness, generosity and instruction in the art of last minute improvisation.